Youth Group: Coming of age in the Church of Christian nationalism is a book that effortlessly blends hilarious personal experiences with serious examination of both the author's motives and the movement in which he was born. People who weren't born and raised in extremist religious movements often find it difficult to understand how totally serious the leaders and followers are about their beliefs. Memoirs like Lance's are a great way to open their eyes. The fight for pluralism and tolerance begins by understanding what their opponents actually think.

Matthew Sheffield, former Mormon and founder of Flux. community

Youth Group

Coming of age in the church
of Christian nationalism

Youth Group

Coming of age in the church of Christian nationalism

Lance Aksamit

Winchester, UK
Washington, USA

JOHN HUNT PUBLISHING

First published by Zero Books, 2023
Zero Books is an imprint of John Hunt Publishing Ltd., No. 3 East St., Alresford,
Hampshire SO24 9EE, UK
office@jhpbooks.com
www.johnhuntpublishing.com
www.zero-books.net

For distributor details and how to order please visit the 'Ordering' section on our website.

Text copyright: Lance Aksamit 2022

ISBN: 978 1 78535 973 6
978 1 78535 974 3 (ebook)
Library of Congress Control Number: 2021947888

A CIP catalogue record for this book is available from the British Library.

Design: Matthew Greenfield

UK: Printed and bound by CPI Group (UK) Ltd, Croydon, CR0 4YY
Printed in North America by CPI GPS partners

We operate a distinctive and ethical publishing philosophy in
all areas of our business, from our global network of authors to
production and worldwide distribution.

Contents

For Anna and Fiadh, who inspire me every day and without whom this book would never have been written.

Acknowledgments

Special thanks to my wife, Anna, who read and reread this manuscript a dozen times and generally managed our entire lives while I slowly plunked at a keyboard. Thanks Lindsay Kerns, Michael Hennings, Laura and Pat Gunther, and Amber Aksamit for helping me develop my voice and keep my history straight. A big thank you to the whole Zero Books team for taking a chance on me and helping me along the way. Thank you to all who contributed their personal stories, it takes real bravery to share difficult and painful memories with strangers. And a heartfelt thank you to my parents, who love me and have always encouraged me to do what is right.

Preface

I never intended for this book to be a book. What began as a personal quest for answers now spans 11 years, some 30-odd countries, and the following pages. Although elements of it were written as far back as 2010, the impetus for what it has become manifested in 2016 with the GOP nomination of Donald Trump. I never expected him to win the election, but his nomination came as no surprise to me. In him I saw what so many of my former compatriots had been longing for. A strongman willing to do whatever it took to restore a lost Christian heritage to America. That wasn't who he actually was, of course, but he spoke directly to Evangelical grievance in a way no politician had before.

I grew up fully immersed in that culture of grievance. I was a white Evangelical. I am still white, but the quest I embarked upon 11 years ago was a deconstruction of my Evangelicalism. I grew up Evangelical, very Evangelical. Like, church every Sunday, Youth Group every Wednesday, Bible camp every summer, Pokemon is the Devil kind of Evangelical. Writing this book began as a search for what made me the way I was. I ran through my past, parsing through events, people, and experiences that had yielded some of the deepest impacts. Having done so, I landed on Youth Group.

This book may read differently than much of the nonfiction you're accustomed to. Blended within is an abstract anthropological take on Evangelical youth culture, a chronological historical analysis, and my semi-chronological personal narrative. I find the result to be a unique, but intuitive, read. *Youth Group* tackles dozens of Evangelicalism's various facets, each could be a book unto itself. As such, it is not intended to be an exhaustive resource on any one of them. Even more elements were omitted than were included. Some on purpose, others by ignorance. These omissions will lead to accusations of cherry-picking history. An inevitable outcome when engaging in a project such as this, but regrettable nonetheless. I focused on the threads of Evangelicalism which I feel best articulate the path taken to arrive at its present state.

While reading this book it may feel as if I am equating all of Christianity with Evangelicalism. I am not. However, as America's predominant religious force, Evangelicalism is treated as Christianity's beloved son. I also chose not to delve into differentiating between Christian nationalism and white Christian nationalism as many of my colleagues have done. This is not to say a distinction does not exist. Also, I chose to include all citations within the text itself, mostly because I hate having to look in the back of a book to find where the information came from.

Be forewarned, *Youth Group* confronts some of Evangelicalism's greatest heroes with an irreverence and humor that some may find distasteful. It also pokes fun at purity culture, Christian sanctimony, conservatism, and Rush Limbaugh. It contains a few opinions and historical interpretations which, although well grounded, may fall short of academic rigor. This book is not intended to be a textbook but, rather, a thought-provoking polemic.

For those who, like me, have exited Evangelicalism there is a lot in here I am sure you'l appreciate. If you were fortunate enough to have been raised absent of any form of fundamentalism, let this book serve as a window into an alien world. For those who still consider themselves Evangelicals, I entice you to read with an open mind and to fact check me if at any point you remain unconvinced. Whoever you are, thank you for buying my book.

Chapter 1

What is Youth Group?

Girls were taught that it was our role in romantic relationships to help maintain the sexual purity of ourselves and our partners. Through taking certain actions, we could prevent boys from acting on their rampant, uncontrollable biological urges hardwired into them by God for procreation. For example, the straps on our tank tops needed to pass the "three-finger" width requirement – anything thinner would cause boys to have impure thoughts. If we went down the slippery slope of physical contact or kissing, it was our duty to prevent things from escalating beyond a kiss because after a certain point, our partner would have no ability to stop himself.

This was true, I found. Through my relationship with the son of a pastor at my church, I discovered that the narrative – male sexual desire was uncontrollable – caused boys to behave in such a way that made the narrative true. On more than one occasion, I witnessed this self-fulfilling prophecy play out and was left to grapple with my own actions in the aftermath: What should I have done when I'd fulfilled my role as "gatekeeper" to the best of my ability and it still wasn't enough? When I had forcefully said "no" and "stop," and he ignored me? When, with all of my strength, I tried to push him off of me and he refused to stop until he was finished?

It has taken a decade of living a secular life to realize there is only one way to describe what my boyfriend had done to me – assault. But in a Christian context, it was complicated. He was the son of a pastor. We were in a relationship. I had agreed to be alone with him while our friends went out. I had allowed the kissing to start.
Sara, Iowa

My heartbeat hovered at a consistent 170, and I had one leg painfully cramped up underneath the other. Acutely aware of how my clammy hands must feel against her bare skin, I advanced. She worked charitably to assist in my quest by pulling both arms out of her sleeves, turning her sweater into a sort of bunchy scarf. Smashed as we were between a leaning stack of hymnals and a rack of choir robes, our position was precarious enough without accounting for the 30 slightly more repressed teenagers who were actively searching for us. The name of the game was sardines, a favorite for obvious reasons, and God bless her church for all night "Lock-ins." Evangelical youth leaders across the country thought these Lock-ins were an absolutely fantastic idea. They would take as many hormone-addled youths as were readily available, pump them full of Mountain Dew, pizza, and oatmeal cream pies then turn off the lights and play oddly provocative games, watch inoffensive movies, and listen to truly terrible music until the rising sun would signal moms in minivans to arrive.

I belonged to a very Christian family in the American Midwest and church Youth Groups provided one of the few venues where loosely supervised commingling was possible. I attended as many as four different Youth Groups a week for this very reason. Looking back, I've noticed a complete lack of creativity in naming these groups. The era when youth-focused associations bore illustrious names such as *The Junior Birdmen of America* or *The Kindred of the Kibbo Kift* were long gone. Often, a church would attempt to stand out by branding their Youth Group with some kitsch Christianese. When those words formed a clever acronym, double points were awarded. At one point, I attended both "The ER" (Extreme Remedy) and a group featuring free coffee called "Holy Grounds." However, no amount of effort in rebranding had any real staying power. Call it what you will; for those who attended, Youth Group went by no other name. As if forged by universal constants, church Youth Groups uniformly developed the same sets of heliocentric social circles. The star in the epicenter was invariably a charismatic, male, 22-year-old graduate from Grace, Crown, Liberty, or Emmaus Christian college. With a degree in "Youth Ministries" fresh in hand, these youth pastors boldly led, and formed the heart of, the Youth Group. Often, a waning crescent of space would be made for their demure wives who would lead girls' groups and occasionally worship.

Expanding outwards, there was the "leadership team": a group of between five and ten future leaders of America who never missed a Youth Group activity (which were inexplicably always on Wednesday nights), Sunday morning service, or any other church function. Usually a decent enough group of kids, but being so close to the sun had the tendency to blind over time. The orbit a bit further out was populated by the "Regulars." Showing up at almost every event and filled with enough rambunctious zeal to keep the entire system spinning, the bulk of the Youth Group found a home in this orb. While I held leadership roles, I chose to primarily reside here. I was as impassioned as anyone, but I despised imposition and obligation, so a Regular I remained. The next concentric circle belonged to the "Irregulars." A more unenviable cadre I cannot imagine. These were the kids who, for one reason or another, did not find a niche at school or church and only made the occasional appearance at Youth Group. Owing their infrequent attendance to being bright enough not to fully buy in but still suffering from a very human need to socialize. When they did make an appearance between extended dry spells, they were greeted with infantile coos and caws from the Regulars, the leadership team, and the youth pastor alike. Like a doting mother praising a child who has finally learned to remove their pants before a shit. The copious and suffocating attention intended to incentivize regular membership served to drive many irregulars back into hiding. The final concentric circle encompassed everyone between the ages of 14 and 19 who somehow managed to both exist and not attend a Youth Group. This demographic held the highest importance. To lure in one or more of these guaranteed status and unimagined notoriety. Primarily because it proved you had friends outside of Youth Group.

Despite its vague, androgynous name, Youth Group had some precise and gendered messages. Often, meetings would be separated by sex, where the girls would read *Captivating*, and the boys would read *Wild at Heart*. In the spirit of togetherness, *I Kissed Dating Goodbye* might be read communally. Boys, you are a slave to your impulses; best not be too close to a girl. Better yet, don't ever be alone with one. Girls, there's nothing more attractive than modesty; if you want a boy to be attracted to you, it's probably because you're some sort of a slut. If any boy does take notice, you share in his sin as did Eve with the apple.

Most importantly, for both boys and girls, there is no appropriate outlet for your sexuality until marriage. Maybe not even then. Messages that stood in stark contrast with at least half of the games played in Youth Group. Passing a playing card from one set of lips to another, groping around unsupervised in dark closets while playing sardines, or attempting to burst a balloon by smashing it between yours and a chosen partner's genitalia. Mixed messages abounded.

Youth Group was not all fun and frolics; the serious business of Bible study did have its place. The youth pastor chose a passage and delivered a condensed sermon with flair and highly suspect testimonials. A song or two would be sung before the leadership team helped break up into small groups. Inside these small groups, members would humbly take turns at one-upping the previous speaker with ever more perceptive takes and brave disclosures.

For young Evangelicals like myself, Youth Group played a more significant role in shaping our worldview than did

any other aspect of attending church. Every Youth Group
I attended, and there were a few, seemed to fit this similar
mold. Unsurprising when any profound divergence from the
straight and narrow could earn you the brand of heretic. I was
enormously invested in my Youth Group but it is hard not to
look back with a tumult of contrasting emotions. There were
wonderful times with kind and loving leaders who provided a
place to belong when belonging was all that most of us wanted.
However, it was also a source of tremendous guilt, fear, and a
sense of constant besiegement.

Any message addressing normal teenage relationships was
tinged with shame and strong currents of sexual repression. On
Thursday mornings, the Youth Group males were encouraged
to meet at Burger King before school and read *Every Man's
Battle: Winning the War on Sexual Temptation One Victory at a Time*
by Stephen Arterburn, then discuss how long it had been since
we masturbated. It was called an "accountability group." No
tangible benefit was even imagined. It was always tied back to
the guilt of disappointing God or our guaranteed and not-at-all
hypothetical future wives. Much later I would find out that this
trend was being carried on at the highest levels of government,
but probably not at a Burger King. More on that to come.

What we men had to bear was nothing compared to the load
carried by the "fairer sex." While jacking off to slowly buffering
"internet porn" denied our future wives exclusive rights to our
coveted boners, a girl's entire worth was on the line. A concept
known in Youth Group simply as "purity." Perhaps best
exemplified by the following iteration of a common metaphor
which was typically presented to the young women by the
youth pastor's wife: "Imagine a rose passed from hand to hand,
with each pass a petal is taken. In no time at all, the rose is
nothing but a stem, and who would want to keep only a thorny
stem?" This efflorescent metaphor wonderfully exposes from
where a girl's value stems, let alone virtue. Other less charitable

metaphors were also employed. Tape covered with lint and hair no longer able to stick, chewed gum swapping from one gaping mouth to another, a communal toothbrush, a glass of water in which all who drank had left copious amounts of saliva, etc. Like the process in *A Clockwork Orange*, purity culture often relied on revulsion, disgust, and shame.

Girls were taught to curse the clitoris and bless the hymen while somehow being taught blessedly little about either. When not resorting to poorly wrought analogy, a less negative yet equally Pavlovian approach was common. "Purity rings" or "Promise Rings" may be the most widely renowned artifacts of purity culture, but other, more extravagant practices existed as well. "Purity balls" were held in church gymnasiums where 13- and 14-year-old girls clad in white dresses were paraded in front of the congregation by their fathers, then pledged themselves and their chastity to their future bridegrooms. An early girlfriend of mine had made a vow in her Youth Group not to kiss anyone until her wedding day. It was not until the stroke of midnight on New Year's Eve when I discovered this hard truth. Purity contracts were signed by both boys and girls. While I have long since forgotten the exact text of the contract I signed, the gist still sticks with me and is as follows:

> I promise to God, my future wife, and myself to save sex for marriage and to keep my mind and body pure so that when I enter the marriage covenant, I will be able to give myself entirely as God intended.

The mind and body purity bit was a euphemism for watching porn and masturbation. No consideration was given to the thought that a girl might want to, or even could, masturbate. Neither was the possibility that either a boy or a girl in the Youth Group might prefer the attentions of anyone other than their biblically prescribed, sexual counterparts. Upon signing the sacred covenant, you received a knowing nod from the youth pastor and a coupon for a free personal pan pizza from Pizza Hut. If the intended goal of purity culture was to get kids to "wait till marriage" then it had mixed results at best. Worse still, the methods left many casualties. I know a girl who believed the act of losing one's virginity to be so life altering and momentous that she was unable to have sex with her husband for almost a year after they were married. I have had conversations with too many people who endured years of abuse, thinking it was their Christian duties. A good friend of mine believed for years that it was her provocative style of dress that led to her sexual assault at a church camp. The pathology for these events is complex, and purity culture is not the only contributing factor. However, each person I spoke to about their experiences firmly connected the two.

In its attempt to warn young Christians about the dangerous alures of sex, purity culture put sex front and center. Everything was about sex in one way or another, bringing attention to then sexualizing things that would have otherwise gone unnoticed. Better cover those three millimeters of exposed bra strap, too sexy. For me, the constant meditations and learned sensitivity simply magnified the hypersexualization already prevalent within American culture at large. As it turns out, ceaselessly worrying about sexual desires boosts sexual desires. I became quite sex obsessed which in turn reinforced my shame causing me to be even more on guard. A terrible cycle. Throw in a handful of misinformation and subtract any form of sexual education and you are left with a guilt-stricken kid afraid he contracted AIDS the first time he masturbated.

Life within Youth Group and the church was posited as a battleground between God and the Devil, light and dark. Grays had no place outside of acceptable non-attention-seeking colors to be worn by women. Christians were the only bulwarks resisting the floodwaters of the antediluvian depravity "the world" yearned to release upon society. "The world" was an Evangelical colloquialism, meaning not only secular humanity, but everyone who was not an Evangelical Christian. The church promoted an unabashed and quite literal "us v.s. the world" mentality. While not necessarily constructive for deeper understanding, this stance did provide endless targets for Jesus's command to "love thy enemy." The separation of church and state was viewed as a moral failing in American history, and events like "See you at the Pole" were constructed to interject Evangelicalism back into schools. Any decline in prominence for Judeo-Christian social norms was greedily attacked with slippery slope logic. Resulting in a future dystopia where marrying your Cocker Spaniel was legal but going to church was not. We fetishized adversity and persecution, giving every perceived slight undue weight. Where even the possible suggestion of offense was missing – it would be conjured up. We imagined countless secret secular cabals all hellbent on destroying Christianity and America. Lacking even windmills, we tilted at shadows.

Maybe this last chapter reads as completely alien to you. If so, bear with me; there is more context to come. If a few connections are sliding into place, or perhaps you are suffering from a bit of deja entendu, do not be overly alarmed. It is almost impossible to turn on the TV or open up YouTube without hearing many of these ideals espoused by protesters and politicians alike. Red MAGA hats did not grow the heads underneath them. Evangelicals are now predominantly Christian nationalists. Those hats and the ideology they represent are merely the latest outward showing of a long prevalent trend. When I watched the Capitol riots on January 6, 2021, I saw all the signs and scars that still crisscross my own thinking. Youth Group alone can't be blamed for where many of its old members have ended up. Yet, when I see faces that I recognize in the crowds on the Capitol steps and read insane posts from people I went to Youth Group with, clear connections aren't hard to come by. What's more, as a one-time recruiter, I cannot help but view the present tensions with a heavy sense of onus.

"But Lance," I can already hear my academically minded colleagues saying, "all of what you're saying is anecdotal and, thus far, unsubstantiated. I need facts, surveys, something more than these tenuous connections." Hopefully the later chapters will quench that thirst, but first it is important to understand a few things.

Chapter 2

The Great Awakening

By the time I moved into my college dorm room, I had somehow accumulated 4 copies of the (manically) popular book I Kissed Dating Goodbye. *One copy to match an overflowing crate of other "purity books" I had organized into a donation/burn pile as I packed my childhood away into moving boxes. This book was one of the cornerstones upon which the purity culture that saturated my church's youth group was built, essentially communicating to us that our sexual purity was the highest gift we could offer the Lord.*
Kayla, Nebraska

As enthralling as it may be to trace the roots of Evangelicalism back through the centuries and across church schisms, I feel that the only people who would actually enjoy that are the same people who complain that an hour of galactic senate hearings was the secret sauce missing from the latest Star Wars. Yes, I know it wouldn't make sense to incorporate the galactic senate as it was disbanded by Palpatine long before *A New Hope*, but still, I'm sticking to the analogy.

Cause and effect can be slippery. Someone wishing to pinpoint any initial cause will be forced into a perpetual retreat through time. That being said, I believe much of the modern Evangelical dogma bestowed upon us in Youth Group can have its origins best understood in the light of four historical events; the Great Awakening, the Civil War, the Russian Counter-Revolution, and the election of Ronald Reagan. The underlying American Puritanism and the religious zealotry of the genocidal first colonists will be taken as a matter of course.

The last time you were forced to read anything about the Great Awakening was most likely 8th grade history class, and it was probably presented in grand but slightly oblique terminology. Depending on the curriculum, it is either taught that the Great Awakening was a culmination of Enlightenment ideals or that the Great Awakening was a reactionary response to those same ideals. Either way, the Great Awakening created a monumental shift in Christendom. Spirited on by wide-roaming laymen preachers, the 1700s saw religious revivals spring up on both sides of the Atlantic. Although the revivalists held onto the Puritan fascination with the end of the world and the Protestant love of work, they introduced a bit of flavor in the form of a highly personal God who loved to communicate via emotional outbursts. This new wave of religiosity had "New Lights" like George Whitefield at the helm. A card-carrying member of the "Holy Club," Whitefield was an English itinerant preacher who was not satisfied with merely winning a few souls in England alone. Like an old-timey John Lennon, Whitefield knew that he really hadn't "made it" until the colonists had embraced him. And, like an old-timey America, welcome him they did.

Whitefield's dynamic preaching drew crowds in the thousands. However, he was not the only show pony in town. The colonies had no problem producing their own revivalists. Jonathan Edwards, founder of Princeton and Whitefield's only competition for dried apple doll impersonator, was one of the most prominent preachers in the New World. Edwards' through and through conviction won him renown as did his trademark "God has a raging hard-on for torturing sinners" sermons which he would deliver in an eerily soft voice. So intense was his fervor that several of his congregation committed suicide when faced with their complete depravity in the face of God's great goodness. One of his most famous sermons contains this charming excerpt: "The wrath of God burns against them, their damnation don't slumber, the pit is prepared, the fire is made ready, the furnace is now hot, ready to receive them, the flames do now rage and glow. The glittering sword is whet, and held over them." Both Edwards and Whitefield stressed the importance of the conversion process as a massive life-altering event. When adherents spoke the magic words and truly believed them in their hearts, the Holy Spirit would fill them and never leave them no matter what future sins they committed. The "New Lights" called converts "born-again believers," a phrase taken from John chapter 3. While most denominations refer to either baptism or conversion as being "born again in Christ," describing yourself as a "born-again Christian" became *the* Evangelical callsign. The primacy of the conversion event is considered a defining attribute of Evangelicalism as is an emphasis on evangelizing or proselytization.

After admiring each other from afar, Edwards and Whitefield met in the autumn of 1740, and it was love at first sight. The unstoppable duo spent the next several years torturing the 13 colonies together. One might assume that the message of a terrifyingly violent God who wants nothing more than to get real personal with you would be a hard pill to sell. It wasn't. Already primed for guilt by Puritanism and excluded from higher learning by circumstance, the colonists ate it up. The dry old book learning offered by the existing clergy couldn't compete. American colonists allowed their passions to take charge and embraced this new, intimate take on Christianity. So impassioned were many revivalists that burning heaps of "ungodly" books became commonplace. Personal connection to God overcame orthodoxy and revelation might strike anywhere. Edwards and Whitefield saw themselves as ushering in Christ's return by creating a godly society, a city on a hill, that would reign for 1000 years. A concept known as "millennialism."

For some, enough time around bonfires and merely burning books became a bit "blasé." Connecticut minister James Davenport, roused or perhaps aroused by the Holy Spirit, once took off and tossed his trousers into the fire. He beseeched his followers to cast off their worldly trappings as well, but the Holy

Ghost was no match for Puritanical modesty, and this event would, unfortunately, mark the end of Davenport's popularity. I can only imagine how spirited a Youth Group would be in a universe where Davenport's teachings, not Edward's, held sway.

Fueled by the pathos of "New Lights" like Whitefield and Edwards, the Great Awakening tilted the religious landscape away from rigid hierarchy and intellectualism and slanted it toward personal revelation and emotionalism. A motif still held onto in today's Evangelicalism. Channeling these New Lights someone in my Youth Group, usually the youth pastor, would put forth the utterance "It's not a religion; it's a relationship," as if they had spoken some new profundity. The earnestness in which this nugget of wisdom would be delivered was enough to make the rest of the group nod and murmur with equal sincerity. Amazing that an aphorism introduced 100 years before the cracking of the liberty bell could still be proffered as a novel break with tradition.

Over time, this very personalized approach merged with the older hierarchies to produce an unholy hybrid. God speaks to everyone, but mostly to the pastors. After all, the closer to God a person is, the more likely they'll have a transcendent hot take on the Gospels.

The messages of accountability, innate worthlessness, guilt, and redemption took on a new and affectional tone while the intellectual and scholarly approaches were met with outright hostility. Whitefield and Edwards were educated men, but this was very much the exception, not the rule, for itinerant preachers. In his book *The Role of Ideology in the American Revolution*, historian John Howe delineates the shift as such:

Men and women who had worshiped for years without result under the guidance of an erudite but undramatic minister, found grace after a few hours at the feet of some wandering apostle. The itinerant was often a layman who had never been to college and knew no Greek, Latin, or Hebrew, but had a way with an audience. If God selected him to do so much without learning, was learning perhaps more a hindrance than a help to true religion? The thought occurred to many converts and was encouraged by the increasingly confident, not to say arrogant, posture of the itinerants. Whitefield had warned broadly against ministers who preached an unknown and unfelt Christ. His followers did not hesitate to name individual ministers as dead of heart, blind teachers of the blind.

The ministers they named "dead of heart" were driven from their posts and even from their towns by their former congregations. A new anti-intellectualism was afoot. When personal revelation is in play, how someone feels about a thing has much more weight than what someone knows. A sentiment keenly felt in my Youth Group. English, math, and physics were all fine, but a step too far in the science or philosophy direction was a step toward danger. Specific authors, entire schools of thought, evolutionary biology, any geology that required Earth to be over 7000 years old, anything alluding to climate change, and Harry Potter were all snares of the Devil.

James Davenport's fiery legacy found a home almost 300 years later at one of my very first Youth Group events. Some may recall a particularly dramatic fad that passed through the Evangelical community known as "cd burning parties." The name was quite literally what the event was about. Kids would bring all of their secular or "worldly" music, toss them in a metal drum, douse them in lighter fluid, and burn them...for God? These cd burning parties would inevitably boost record sales for the immolated music. As most of the junior arsonists would repurchase the very cd on Thursday that they had burned on Wednesday.

Chapter 3

The Beginning

Youth group and Bible studies also showed me how to be a woman of God and prepare myself for marriage. Being a strong, independent woman was left at the door. My church made it clear that the man was to be the leader in the relationship, and the household, and the church. He was the provider, the protector, and the final decision maker. The woman's role was to support him, follow him, and take care of the family. All of this was backed by verses, sermons, books, and small group discussions. This line of thought was accepted by the majority of the youth, and reinforced by stories of older siblings marrying young and abiding by that lifestyle.
It was in high school I was familiarized with "ring by spring," where women go to college to try to get engaged by spring semester. It seemed that for some women, the whole point of going to college was to find a husband. They get married while in college, then start families right away, never using their degree.
Tricia, Colorado

I was welcomed into the world by the astute doctors of Patilla Hospital in the Central American country of Panama as my parent's fourth niña. A lush head of hair was the culprit for the misgendering, not the lack of male genitalia, no matter what my oldest sister would later claim.

My world was composed of two authoritarian regimes—one political and the other ontological. General Manuel Antonio Noriega Moreno, whose childhood acne scars earned him the whispered nickname of Old Pineapple Face, was the Panamanian autocrat, and Jesus was the benevolent dictator in my home. These two authoritarian regimes would soon find themselves at odds in the backwater jungles of the Darien. Noriega, a violent thug and drug runner who was trained by the US at Fort Bragg and remained a CIA asset for years, finally fell out of Uncle Sam's good graces when he took a less-than-obsequious tone with Washington. The general never trusted his overlords, and when embarrassing connections between him and President George H.W. Bush began appearing in American newspapers, his paranoia was validated. Old Pineapple Face had outlived his usefulness and quickly became a persona non grata.

Ally turned enemy, and a full purge of all suspected American operatives in the country was undertaken. One such suspected agent was my blind, missionary father. My mom and dad, along with my three older sisters and myself, lived past the edge of civilization among the Embera tribe. My parents were in the process of translating the Bible into the local dialect when the general's goons appeared and ransacked our tiny hut. Finding an old two-way radio they claimed to be illegal, the men took my father at gunpoint into the sweltering jungle. I can only imagine the panic my mother felt in the following days without word of my father's whereabouts. The local police would not so much as acknowledge my father's disappearance, and the government was even less forthcoming. The first my mother knew that my father was still alive was when he called from Miami airport a week later. Apparently, a brave, blind missionary with a tendency to recite scripture was a little more than these lackeys had bargained for.

Without an education to fall back on, my parents found clerical work at the missionary "boot camp" that had deployed them to Panama 4 years earlier. It was a strict, no-nonsense fundamentalist Christian commune in Wisconsin where a hundred or so soon-to-be missionaries were versed in both theology and the practical skills needed to survive in far-flung jungles. Women were not allowed to teach anyone, except for small children, nor were they allowed to wear pants. Neither men nor women were allowed to go to the movies, dance, or play cards. In this city upon a hill, it was of utmost importance to flee from even the appearance of evil – which, as we all know, women's pants in the early 90s definitely were. While my mother was once a wild child and my father a pot dealer in high school, they embraced the provided structure and passed it down to their five children.

The leadership of the commune provided daily Bible lessons from kindergarten onwards. One such lesson taught me that my favorite color could not be black. I remember a man with wild red hair and a pockmarked face explaining the ineffable logic by using a little beaded bracelet. "Black is the color of sin, but green represents growth in God and red Jesus' blood." I still recall his pinched voice conveying this message almost as a reprimand. The bracelet contained white, purple, and yellow beads as well but I have since forgotten what he had to say about their significance. I stopped focusing on what he had to say shortly after I was made aware that my favorite color was the Devil's color. Then and there I decided my new favorite color would be green.

The perils of ever-present spiritual warfare were pressed upon us. My older sister became convinced, then convinced me, that my dad was the Antichrist. The result of an age-appropriate lesson on Armageddon where she was helpfully informed that the Antichrist, who could be anyone, would seem very nice at first but was actually concealing the ultimate evil. My father seemed pretty nice, so he fitted the bill. We watched him with considerable scrutiny for several weeks before we cleared him of suspicion. We were also on the lookout for demon possession in both each other and our stuffed animals. An entirely predictable outcome of children being taught that demons could possess anything *except* a true Christian. A fear of demon possession and a fear of burning forever in hell combined to create an ironclad resolution in me to be one of those "true Christians."

Toward this effort I prayed daily to be "born again" for

several years until my mom explained it was more of a one and done kinda deal. When I was about 5 years old, I ran into the kitchen where my mother sat hunched over a newspaper cutting out coupons. She looked up from her task and must have seen the anguish in my face because she put down her scissors and quickly pulled me into her lap. This being a regular occurrence she didn't ask me what the matter was; she simply held me until my balling subsided into hiccups. Grief stricken, I began to confess my latest transgression. "I had a bad thought again," I said, unwilling to divulge more without being asked. "What was it?" my mother asked, probably for the thirty-third time that week. "I thought about kissing on the mouth," I said, with my face to the ground. See, my earlier fear of being flayed alive in the lake of fire for eternity had morphed into an even more devastating concern, disappointing Jesus. I developed a Jungian complex where if I did not confess every misdeed and sinful thought to my mother, I would have panic attacks. She understandably mistook these confessions to be a sign of a sensitive and tender heart, not one of absolute terror. She did rescue me by telling me that I would feel better if, instead of telling her, I told Jesus and only confessed the "big ones" to her. Released from my physical absolutions, much of my fear eventually dissipated but not the associated guilt; that wouldn't subside for another 25 odd years.

My parents were by far and away the least conservative workers at the bootcamp. They routinely got in trouble for pushing boundaries and arguing with leadership. Whenever my mother would leave the property of the commune, she would drive a couple miles down the road then pull over and strip off her *Little House on the Prairie* skirt before pulling on a pair of blue jeans. My father would go to bat for us kids on a regular basis. My four sisters were looked down upon as undisciplined and I was considered far too rambunctious. When the commune leadership piled into our living room one evening to demand the treehouse we had built over the course of a year be torn down, he stood his ground. I sneaked from my room where I had been banished upon their arrival. At the top of the stairs I recall peering around the wall and down at the committee of stern looking men discussing the future of everything my 6-year-old heart cared about. I was so proud that my dad was not afraid of these men who terrified me. Despite my father's reasoned defense, the treehouse was pulled down in the following days.

Yet unmarred by Rush Limbaugh or Fox News, but still an outspoken critic of Democrats and "liberalism", my father shared a bit of wisdom with me, which he might now decry as socialist propaganda. I was about 6 or 7 and sitting in Sunday school where a small mousy woman with frizzy hair told us the parable about the workers in the vineyard. For those who are unfamiliar, I'll lay out a brief synopsis. The owner of a vineyard hired some laborers to work the entire day for a silver Denarius. Most of the day goes by, and the owner contracts several other workers. At the end of the day, all the workers were paid the same silver Denarius no matter when they started to work. The laborers who had been hired first were upset that the latecomers were paid the same as they were.

I was on the side of the angry laborers and said as much to my parents on the car ride home. That's when my dad told me something that made quite the subconscious impact, "Life's not fair, and sometimes that's a good thing. Don't be mad if someone else was given something you worked harder for, be glad they have what they need."

Against the oncoming tide of a very real Jesus-induced neurosis stood the unconditional love of my parents and an almost limitless freedom of play. All the commune's children were left relatively unsupervised for outrageously long stints each day. While this arrangement led to terrible consequences for some, I believe it to have been my deliverance. The property on which we lived had a treasure trove of explorable orchards, hedges, barns, timber yards, junkyards, and a complex network of abandoned tunnels leftover from a clandestine prohibition era distillery. All of which set the scene for uncounted pirate battles, dramas, train robberies, and all-around tomfoolery. Without such, I do not think my mind would have ever escaped the chest in which it was intended to be buried.

By the time I was old enough to go to Youth Group on Wednesday nights, I had already consumed enough Evangelical marketing that violently graphic phrases like "covered by the blood of Jesus" or "washed by the blood of the Lamb" were no more terrifying than a Sunday afternoon potluck. Not so for the uninitiated. I brought an acquaintance from school to Youth Group on a night where the main course was salvation and damnation. She left that night unconvinced her eternal soul was in peril but thoroughly convinced my sanity was.

Each concentric ring of the Youth Group was exposed to variants of the same fear-infused messages. The level of subtlety, and alarm, was directly correlated with the proximity to the sun. Starting outwards and moving in: the irregular had the dangers of secularism, drugs, sex, and the "wrong crowd" delicately pressed upon them, and naturally, the slight matter of eternal damnation. For the uninitiated "irregular," this was a tough sell and rarely won any converts. Consequently, the litany of games, treats, and brotherly love was applied to better entice them into dropping a revolution nearer.

For the "regular," a world threaded with snares and snarls was more vividly depicted. Drugs were not only bad for your health or wellbeing; they were the Devil's way of distracting you from your heavenly duties. Sex was Jesus' chief contender and Satan's sharpest hook. The wrong crowd, however, became a more nuanced topic. While always on your guard against being "led astray," we were not to be overly standoffish with the denizens from the other side of the ethereal tracks. They were the soil in which we were to plant the holy seeds of the gospel. An oft applied parable seemingly ready made for sexually repressed teens who synchronously feared and desired nothing more than to plant some seed.

Of hell and damnation, messages varied depending on denomination and fundamentalist tendency. At a Youth Group I regularly attended, we were treated to an audio recording from Bill Wiese's revelatory book, 23 Minutes in Hell. A book that plays the spectral counterpart in theme and authenticity, if not unambiguous exploitation, to The Boy Who Came Back from Heaven. In it, Wiese fumbles to describe, you guessed it, a 23-minute jaunt in the underworld where he is subjected to beatings and tortures administered by two "creatures," presumably demons, with "the strength approximately one thousand times greater than a man." While the number 23 must have been chosen for its talismanic numerology, Mr Wiese falls back on this "thousand times" trope as regularly as a third-grade schoolboy trumping up the strength of his father after mumbling about how "my dad could beat your dad up." Thrice in consecutive paragraphs, it reappears:

It was absolutely disgusting, foul, and rotten. It was, by far, the most putrid smells I have ever encountered. If you could take every rotten thing you can imagine, such as an open sewer, rotten meat, spoiled eggs, sour milk, dead rotting animal flesh, and sulfur, and magnify it a thousand times, you might come close. This is not an exaggeration.

Followed directly by, "Instinctively, I just knew that some of the things I experienced were a thousand times worse than what would be possible on the earth's surface."

This modern-day Dickensian Job was plunged into, then briskly rescued from, hell by none other than Jesus himself. Ostensibly to provide Mr Wiese with the requisite vocabulary and precise numerical multiplier by which to effectively communicate the novel message that hell is a bad place. His creatures, seemingly torn directly from a Bosch canvas or perhaps out of the mines of Gorgoroth, are thus cheerfully described:

> Each giant beast resembled a reptile in appearance but took on human form. Their arms and legs – unequal in length, out of proportion—without symmetry. The first one had bumps and scales all over its grotesque body. It had a huge protruding jaw, gigantic teeth, and large sunken-in eyes. This creature was stout and powerful, with thick legs and abnormally large feet. It was pacing violently around the cell like a caged bull, and its demeanor was extremely ferocious. The second beast was taller and thinner, with very long arms and razor-sharp fins that covered its body. Protruding from its hands were claws that were nearly a foot long. Its personality seemed different from the first being. It was certainly no less evil, but it remained rather still.

That Mr Wiese considers standing still to be a personality trait might be illuminating in some way, but that must remain a consideration for another time. My prolonged focus on Mr Wiese's *Divine Comedy* may be nearing mean-spirited; however, I believe one more lengthy passage is due. While absurdly humorous, remember the forum in which this was being presented and to whom.

> The second beast, with its razor-like claws and sharp protruding fins, then grabbed me from behind in a bear hug. As it pressed me into its chest, its sharp fins pierced my back. I felt like a rag doll in its clutches in comparison to his enormous size. He then reached around and plunged his claws into my chest and ripped them outward. My flesh

hung from my body like ribbons as I fell again to the cell floor. These creatures had no respect for the human body—how remarkably it is made. I have always taken care of myself by eating right, exercising, and staying in shape, but none of that mattered as my body was being destroyed right before my eyes.

Again, an odd elucidation, taking the time to mention his shapely figure. Time and place suggest more critical considerations. Although his addition isn't as out of place as all that. A man who believes himself God's own emissary of secret knowledge taking the time mid-torture for a trivial boast isn't exactly straying far from the spike tape. As enjoyable as it would be to relay quote after quote from this Wiseau-esque thriller, I believe the point has been adequately made. An account so fantastically come by, and clearly fraudulent, was presented to a group of malleable minds as a reasonable rationale for continuing regular attendance in Youth Group.

Not only did the tightest orbit in the Youth Group solar system face all the aforementioned mongering, but they were also dealt the double blow of having to internalize and repeat it themselves. It was the leadership team that organized and primarily populated the early morning accountability groups. Theirs was the calling to lead by example. Which translated to enjoying, or at least appearing to, countless bizarre games, feeling more guilty for sinful shortcomings, and bearing the brunt of rejection when Youth Group numbers faltered, or a particular event was underpopulated.

The fear of "the world" of which we were to be "in but not of" was manifested in various ways, some more nuanced than others. The ever-raging culture war was never without representation, as was the constant threat of "spiritual warfare." Mayhaps I am being too gracious in separating the former from the latter. Pastors and politicians alike placed, and place, the culture war firmly in the realm of the supernatural. The founder of The Heritage Foundation and father of modern conservatism, Paul Weyrich, described the state of American morality in 1999 as "an ever-widening sewer" and declared the battle already won by "the enemy." As with Harry Potter's "He who shall not be named" "the enemy" is a euphemism for the Devil, and in Mr Weyrich's case, liberals, atheists, socialists, and sometimes the Jews. Mr Weyrich was a pro-life conservative Catholic who coined the term "moral majority" to describe the predominance of American righteousness. Part-time charlatan and full-time dead guy Jerry Falwell would later claim the name for the Evangelical political activist organization that put Reagan in the White House.

Like a local news station endlessly warning parents about some new fad that could be putting their children's lives at risk but isn't really, Evangelicalism, and by extension Youth Group, called for constant defense against the black arts. Everyone talks about the "Satanic Panic" of the 80s but for God's chosen, the Satanic Panic never fell out of vogue. The seductive draws of witchcraft and other insidious demonic messages were so cleverly infused into popular culture as to be almost undetectable. To the vigilant, these pitfalls could be navigated with great care. And, like the emperor's new clothes, when you didn't see them, the correct course of action was to proclaim their existence all the more loudly.

Such vigilance restricted my access to many seemingly harmless things. Harry Potter, Dungeons and Dragons, Pokemon, books on UFOs, and Care Bears were all off limits. Those colorful bears may appear innocent enough, but their new-age emphasis on cooperation over individualism would surely lead to widespread collectivization of farmland then directly to famine and starvation. Or worse, homosexuality. Pokemon was even more dangerous. Pastor Phil Arms, who enjoyed brief notoriety a few years back when one of his sermons lambasting Pokemon received a musical remix on YouTube, wrote the definitive text on the subject. His 2000 book, *Pokemon and Harry Potter: A Fatal Attraction*, currently listed on Amazon for the bargain price of $178.54, provides an unnerving example of the demonic nature inherent to a particular Pokemon, "The Pokemon Psyduck has incredible telepathy or mental powers. Too bad he thinks they are his own and does not realize it is actually demons that empower him." One cannot help but question if Mr Arms is aware of Psyduck's fictional status.

Needless to say, D&D was an even more apparent doorway to the occult because of wizards and stuff, but it had been denounced by the church since the 70s. The new threat was Harry Potter, also containing wizards, and it churned even more choler in the spleens of Evangelicals than its role-playing predecessor. Perhaps it was due to its seemingly innocuous veneer. A video created by Patrick Matrisciana, which made its rounds through churches and Youth Groups in the early 2000s, issued a stark warning that Harry Potter was itself a direct doorway to hell.

If Mr Matrisciana's name tickles a memory, it may be his connection to the aforementioned Jerry Falwell. Together these two created the *Clinton Chronicles* in which Falwell interviewed a reporter whose secret knowledge of the Clintons was so damning as to require only his blacked-out silhouette to be disclosed. Unsurprisingly, this "reporter" turned out to be Mr Matrisciana himself, the producer, and co-financier of the film and a man whose person, he later admitted, was not at all at risk of encountering a Clinton-commissioned bullet. He was also the man responsible for the paid testimonies in "Troopergate" and a primary force behind the Vince Foster conspiracy theory. An all-consuming hatred of the Clintons and a dizzying obsession with demonic cabals was not something unique to Mr Matrisciana or even Mr Falwell. However, they were among the vanguard, and the conspiracy culture they hawked in 1993 still permeates Evangelicalism and right-wing politics today.

Mr Matrisciana and his production company Jeremiah Films produced hundreds of films with topics ranging from Satan being the puppet master behind Mormonism, to meditation being a path to Satan, to birthday magicians pulling Satan out of a hat, to evolution being Satan's hoax, and let's not forget the film that brought us here: *Harry Potter: Witchcraft Repackaged*, which described Harry Potter as the "latest tool being used to disciple children into the darkest aspects of black magic." Previous tools presumably included fairy tales, music with drums, and whatever voodoo makes a microwave work. Affecting a seriousness found only in documentaries played by substitute teachers, the narrator continues with this ominous warning, "Children, as young as kindergarten age, are being introduced to human sacrifice." As if the fundamentalist Christian author had never subjected his children to the crucifixion of the Nazarene. Meanwhile, *Lord of the Rings* and *The Chronicles of Narnia* remained whitelisted despite their wizards or ritual sacrifice.

Anything that dared push against Christian hegemony quickly found itself the object of Evangelical ire. I recall campaigns to shut down everything from JCPenny to the Teletubbies. We were cancel-culture hipsters, sanctimoniously canceling things long before the Left appropriated our tawdry piety. We also helped pioneer modern identity politics. We split the world into oppressed Christians and oppressive secularists. Before the petit bourgeois declared doubting the existence of the patriarchy to be an uncontested sign of internalized sexism, we had long since done that with the Devil. Self-flagellating moralism? Yeah, we did that first too. It seems to me, every ideological purity test now employed by the Left has a religious predecessor. As with today's liberals, Evangelicals of my youth were sated by vapid exchanges in the culture wars, leaving the complicated material roots of those wars relatively unaddressed.

The culture wars were at peak hysteria in the early aughts and encompassed just about everything. Hostilities usually ramped up around Christmas. At Youth Group in November and December, there would be countless small group sessions where the "reason for the season" would be hashed and rehashed. Commercialism and superficiality be damned, God's only begotten son had nothing to do with this or that sale and should not be used as some department store cutout hawking scarves and nativity sets. Once the entire congregation was properly enraged at the commodification of our Lord and savior, a seemingly antithetical outrage would follow suit. How dare the very same carpetbaggers employ a "happy holidays" or "season's greetings" instead of the traditional "Merry Christmas!" Macy's better keep Christ in Christmas even if in so doing, they are doing that exact thing I wished seconds earlier that they would not do! Even Christmas ditties whose authors hadn't had the decency to add a line or two about mangers and Wise Men were held in some contempt.

Music has always played a particularly troublesome role for Christians. Somewhere between confusing a neighborhood kid shouting with the voice of God and delineating original sin, St Augustine found music so enrapturing as to warrant the now-famous utterance "I have become a problem to myself." Where Augustine blamed himself, later Christians shifted the fault to a much more comfortable location: the music itself. The late 90s and 00s were no exception. A fear that demonic forces were backward-masking "heil satans" onto albums was commonplace. "Secular" music was either harboring occult messaging or was far too obscene for Christian consumption and sometimes both. Neither the Gorillaz nor Mariah Carey were allowed into my home and were played only through headphones when on Youth Group retreats. I once had a youth pastor warn me that listening to Destiny's Child was like "putting Satan in a bottle and pouring him into your ear." To be fair, his particular disdain of Queen B and co stemmed from a misheard lyric. He thought the line from Jumpin Jumpin' "The club is full of ballers and their pockets full grown" was "The club is full of ballers and their cocks are full grown." Hearing a grown man explain the wickedness of a line that never existed while saying the word "cock" several times to a room full of teenagers remains a precious memory for me.

While it can be convincingly argued that the Pentecostals inadvertently invented rock n' roll by saturating impressionable youths like Elvis, B.B. King, Jerry Lee Lewis, James Brown, and Little Richie with upbeat tempos and sick guitar riffs, it was the mainstream Evangelicals who tried to kill it. First by censorship and moral outrage, then with appropriation. By the late 90s, Christian music had reached a new derivative low. While I will always have a disco-lit corner in my heart reserved for Five Iron Frenzy, DC Talk, and Newsboys it is impossible to argue that their "secular" counterparts were not markedly superior. My Youth Group dealt in the worst of these artists. It was the music you can still find today somewhere in the 90-megahertz range on any radio across America. You know the ones I'm talking about, the music that within seconds you can easily tell is "Christian music." A discernment that can be made even before any lyrics are sung. It is kind of like how moviegoers find CGI faces in live-action films to be off-putting no matter how lifelike they appear. Grand Moff Tarkin notwithstanding. It is almost as if we are subconsciously biased against imitations. In the immortal words of Hank Hill, "Can't you see you're not making Christianity better, you're just making rock n' roll worse."

As a child, music was less of something to be enjoyed and more of something to be dreaded. The radio's primary purpose was to play Paul Harvey and later Rush Limbaugh. Our seldom-used cassette deck was mostly employed as an auditory pail of cold water to rouse all five children out of bed to do chores on Saturdays. The greatest injustice done to sheet music was the mandatory holiday pageants held by my Christian school and church alike. These pageants were rehearsed to military precision and instilled in me a distrust of both organized religion and music teachers. There was the rare treat when, in the car, my parents would play an Acapella or a Steve Green cassette, or even better, we would listen to recordings of Ranger Rick, Adventures in Odyssey, Patch the Pirate, Unshackled, or Solomon the Supersonic Salamander on the radio. If you are unfamiliar with at least two of the radio programs mentioned above, there is a good chance you were a well-adjusted teenager in high school.

The same injustice done to music was done to all other aspects of everyday life. There is an Evangelical "rule 34" of sorts. If it exists in the secular world, there's an Evangelical version. When I went to private Christian school or when I was homeschooled, my life existed entirely within an Evangelical bubble. I would listen to awful Christian music in the mornings. I would then go to school where every class had an Evangelical slant, including science class, where I watched Kent Hovind explain that man coexisted with the T-rex. That the Earth was once encompassed by an ice wall called the firmament, which kept oxygen levels on Earth extremely high. The high oxygen allowed for pre-flood people to live for hundreds of years and for dinosaurs to grow to enormous size. As a young child, I even had a coloring book that featured dinosaurs with saddles and baby stegosaurus entering the ark to escape the flood. One day we even watched a video claiming Noah's Ark had been found in Iraq, but the discovery was being hidden by Islamists who feared the discovery would validate Christianity. That the flood is also featured in the Quran seemed to have slipped through the editorial process.

Driving home from school, I would listen to right-wing talk radio. Once in the house, I would read Christian fantasy novels.

Then on to Youth Group in the evenings. Christian movies are so bad that even my parents did not insist upon watching them. However, they did purchase a TVGuardian. The TVGuardian would mute the audio whenever a curse word was said. It would replace the sentence containing the expletive with subtitles where the offending word would be switched with a less objectionable one. For example, the word "sex" would be replaced by "hugs," "fuck," with "wow," and "dick," with "jerk." Context never mattered, causing the Richard Nixon documentary on PBS to be even more disparaging than intended. It also caused fellow students to give me sidelong glances when I laughed too loudly at the anti-drug posters put up in the hallways, which read "hugs, not drugs!" Exploring anything too far outside of the Evangelical bubble resulted in stern warnings from authority figures. It was common for children born on this island to spend their entire lives there. Indoctrination of the young was viewed as a parent's Christly duty. What real benefit is there to teaching a healthy skepticism or encouraging intellectual curiosity if it might lead to damnation?

Youth Group regularly combined all the worst aspects of the Evangelical bubble; bad music, bad theology, and bad Christian movies. On a cold February evening in 2004, the Extreme Remedy Youth Group took an outing to the East Park Cinema. Solemnly, we snaked through the rows to our assigned seats. Like millions of other Americans that weekend, we had paid $10 a ticket to see Jesus being tortured and killed. A passion project of Mel Gibson, who was still a reputable actor and director at the time, *The Passion of the Christ* grossed over 370 million dollars in the US alone. The audience is not spared a second of excruciating and graphic detail. The unblinking depiction of flesh being ripped from the Messiah's back is particularly memorable. Mel Gibson directed and financed the film. Although to hear Mel tell it, he did not direct the movie at all, the Holy Ghost did. Mel's apparent dislike of the Jews could be guessed at even before his drunken ramblings, and more than a hint of it exists in the film. None of which should be surprising as he belongs to a bizarre Catholic sect that rejects the Pope's authority and decries the second Vatican council as heretical. Vatican II was where the church finally decided the Jewish people no longer bore the taint of deicide. This was in 1962. Mel was very close with his father, a holocaust denier, fellow crazy-church congregant, and somehow a Jeopardy grand champion. Apparently, the Holy Ghost didn't have all the details straight because Mel also lists the long-dead nuns Catherine Emmerich and Mary of Agreda as sources for the script. This is of note because Mary believed Jewish guilt "descended to their posterity and even to this day continue[s] to afflict this group with horrible impurities." Not to be outdone, Catherine claimed to have rescued "an old Jewess Myer" from purgatory who paid for her rescue by admitting that Jews would regularly strangle Christian children and use their entrails for "all sorts of suspicious and diabolical purposes." Which leads me to speculate on the unsuspicious use of Christian entrails. Catherine also claimed there were unicorns living freely in the Himalayas. Having provided such marvelous revelations, it's no wonder Pope John Paul II beatified Catherine Emmerich the very year *The Passion of the Christ* was released. Clearly, neither the rest of the Extreme Remedy nor I knew any of this at the time.

The movie ended, and we all sat in silence until the last credit rolled by. We maintained our silence back up the aisle, out the theater doors, and into the 15-passenger church van. Uncomfortable, I started to say something but was promptly hushed by my youth pastor. Another 5 minutes of mourning while we sat unbuckled in the van. Finally, he must have decided the moment was sufficiently infused with solemnity and weight because he broke the silence with a benediction. "Jesus endured all of that for each of us. If only one of us were alive on earth, he still would have died to save us. That's how much he loves us,

31

and that is the consequence of our sin." As if to punctuate his statement, he turned the keys in the ignition and started the van back to the church.

Evangelicalism and right-wing politics were already becoming inseparable by the time I entered Youth Group. Fox News dominated the ratings, and characters like Bill O'Reilly, Sean Hannity, and Glenn Beck ruled the airwaves. I grew up listening to all 4 hours of Rush Limbaugh's radio program with the occasional Hugh Hewitt, Michael Medved, or Dennis Pragur thrown in for good measure. It is almost impossible to sufficiently stress how transformative the right-wing echo chamber was for the Evangelical world, especially with Rush Limbaugh at its head. When God recently repoed the talent he had loaned Rush for 70 years it created a vacuum of cigar smoke and vitriol. Risking vulgarity, I do see poetic justice, of a sort, at play. A man spending his entire career spewing cancerous hate and chauvinism from his throat only to die of throat cancer? Well, it speaks for itself. Whatever gastropod or, more likely, gastropods fill Limbaugh's vacated shell will find an audience ready and waiting.

Entire libraries have been dedicated to deciphering the intricacies of the right-wing media's success, so I'll be terse. Somehow, despite being the most watched and most listened to programs, they all claimed not to be the "mainstream media." In this way, and many others, the Evangelical world mirrored the right-wing political one. My family only listened to Christian FM stations and right-wing AM stations. Usually, I couldn't tell which was which. Both were obsessed with real and imaginary foes. Each pushed the narrative that America was falling apart, and the liberals were to blame. Evangelicals ate a steady diet of fear on Sunday mornings from the pulpit, Sunday nights from the cable news, weekday mornings from talk radio, then again weeknights back on the TV. So much information and so little of it useful. The closest thing I ever heard to a critique of a neoliberal principle was the entirely fabricated story that liberals banned harmless CFCs so they could reap the benefits of selling an alternative propellant.

My parents had not grown up in this world. They were ex-rockers from Nebraska who cut their teeth on Ozzy Osborne, Led Zeppelin, and KISS. Their conversion to Christianity came with an almost absolute abandonment of their former lifestyle. Not exactly sure what made music "godly" or "worldly," they opted to err on the side of caution and shun most music found outside a hymnal. I cannot be too upset that I wasn't allowed access to "Stairway to Heaven" or "Rock and Roll All Nite." In their minds they were trying to protect my eternal soul.

Chapter 4

Left Behind

When I first read that eighty percent of white evangelicals had voted for Donald Trump in the 2016 presidential election – ultimately leading him to victory – I was shocked. I had left the church in an ugly breakup ten years prior but for the first twenty years of my life I had been deeply immersed in that world as the daughter of an Assemblies of God minister. I'd already set a pretty low bar of expectations for the church after that experience but this overwhelming show of support for a man who seemed to go against everything they believed was not something I had seen coming. For all of their faults, evangelicals were still the community who had raised me. They were the same people who had taught me that lying, bullying and racism were wrong. The same people who preached against greed, lust and pride. Who said God was grieved by those things, so we should be grieved by them as well. This felt like a betrayal and it didn't make sense. Not at first.
Ryssa, Oregon

Few Dispensational precepts grip the Evangelical imagination or arouse their carnal appetites more than the belief that the world will end in fire and bloodshed. And that it will happen soon. A 2010 Pew survey found that 41 percent of Evangelicals believe the end times will occur before 2050. While not precisely standard fare at most Youth Group events, a spirit of greedy anticipation would take the room whenever the topic was broached. Terms like pre-trib, mid-trib, post-trib, the rapture, the mark of the beast, the Millennial Kingdom, the 70 weeks of Daniel, and of course the Whore of Babylon were passed around in lieu of Pokemon cards as a handful of high-minded teenagers would casually discuss the slaughter of all mankind by a loving

God. Each one of us replete with sanctimonious glee as we sat contemplating a final "I told you so."

A series of 16 books, many of which topped a 100k word count, were authored to both capitalize on and englut the apocalyptic bloodlust. The first book, *Left Behind*, was published in 1995 and within a few scant years was accepted by most Evangelicals as the Bible part deux. Written by Tim LaHaye and Jerry B. Jenkins and selling over 80 million copies, the *Left Behind* series managed to mate Evangelical's martyr complex with strict biblical reconstructionism. The resulting *Rosemary's Baby* maintained the New York Times Best Seller top spot for 7 weeks. No mean accomplishment for a book that was terribly reviewed and contains more than its fair share of truly toilsome dialog.

Mr Jenkins appears to have done the actual writing while the intellectual content was pried from Mr LaHaye's imagination. The plot follows men like Rayford Steele and Buck Williams. Names seemingly snatched from the folds of a sparkling Chippendale's man thong. The protagonists are faced with a world turned upside down by the disappearance of all the true Christians. Pilots vacuumed to heaven mid-flight, doctors mid-surgery, and, presumably, dog walkers mid-dog walk. The rapture has called all the followers of Christ to heaven leaving their clothing, jewelry, fillings, and pacemakers in heaps on the spots where they last stood. The majority of Catholics are mentioned explicitly as having missed the call. Apparently, Martin Luther was on to something after all. But not to fear! Those having been *Left Behind* can still make their way into God's good graces and find their way to heaven via a tedious, long-winded 16-book franchise.

Following the mainstream Dispensational belief, *Left Behind* posits the end times as following exact biblical formulas; prophesied events bring about the rapture, followed by the Great Tribulation. The tribulation consists of war, famine, pestilence, and death—typical apocalyptic horsemen stuff. Finally, after

Jesus' blood lust is quenched, the Millennial Kingdom is installed on Earth for 1000 years where Christ reigns supreme from his throne in Jerusalem. After 1000 years, God remembers he hasn't delivered enough punishments and destroys the Earth with fire before his final judgment begins. Reject the "free gift" of salvation, or simply born in the wrong place at the wrong time? Eternal damnation. Confess with your mouth and believe in your heart that Jesus Christ is king? Eternal bliss in heaven.

The series can be viewed as little more than cathartic revenge porn. Offering the elicit hope that soon all those bearded intellectuals and evolution peddling atheists will finally and violently come face to face with how very wrong they were the whole time. The ejaculative release of seeing several billion naysayers being burned alive for eternity was too much for many of us to pass by.

The series soon exploded off the page and into film, comic books, and video games. If you have yet to experience one of these movies, please start with the Kirk Cameron rendition before moving onto the 2014 Nicholas Cage masterpiece. One does not drink a fine wine before cleansing the palate after all. The franchise offers plenty of guilt-free murder and gore. After a particularly graphic battle where "Men and women and soldiers and horses seemed to explode where they stood," The Lamb of God surveys his work strolling through the carnage with "the hem of his robe turning red in the blood of the enemy." I mean, if Jesus is doing the smiting, it can't be wrong, right?

Keeping track of the good guys and bad guys in *Left Behind* gives you an eerily prophetic look into the Christian nationalist hivemind of today. Top of the list, the United Nations, NATO, Europeans, Muslims, liberals, atheists, humanists, the media, and international bankers. He couldn't be forthright and say George Soros and the Rothchilds. Perhaps even more telling, the good guys include American right-wing militias, some nice Jews, presumably none of which are bankers, and, of course, born-again Evangelicals.

As with glitter, herpes, and Coronavirus, Mr LaHaye refused to be contained. Death cult fanfiction was not his only contribution to the culture wars. Remember Mr Falwell and the Moral Majority from a few pages back? Yeah, Mr LaHaye was instrumental with its formation, and he sat on the three-person board of directors. He was also the founder of the secretive far-right Council for National Policy (CNP), whose membership includes senators, attorneys general, presidential cabinet members, televangelists, and billionaire war criminals. Unlike Falwell's Moral Majority, which folded in the 80s, the CNP continues to meet three times a year in undisclosed locations and has its fingers in almost every level of government. To give you some idea of the power Mr LaHaye wielded; in 2000, presidential hopeful George W. Bush walked into a room with Mr LaHaye without the Evangelical vote and walked out with it entirely behind him.

Mr LaHaye died in 2016, but he had played an almost unparalleled role in pushing conspiratorial beliefs into mainstream Evangelicalism before his departure. A staunch believer in the Illuminati's global dominance and the inherent villainy of the UN, LaHaye helped turn up Evangelical fear to 11. The idea that international liberal elites are determined to crush Christianity, destroy America, and erase Western civilization is Evangelical orthodoxy. *Left Behind* was an addictive and not-so-subtle piece of propaganda that was mainlined to young Evangelicals across the country, myself included.

"The Bible tells us that Jesus will not return until every ear has heard and tongue confessed that Jesus Christ is Lord, and that's one reason missions are so important," intoned my 25-year-old youth pastor, his messianic bearded visage offset by his ever-present cargo shorts. Come to think of it, he bore a slight resemblance to a more saintly John Goodman via *The Big Lebowski*. Nine of us lounged in old sofas, soaking up the seriousness of our impending mission trip to Haiti. While Haiti had already seen its fair share of missionaries and was worse for it, our discussion that night concerned missions in a much broader sense. An air of solemn intensity burned in his eyes as he continued, "And he said unto them, 'go into all the world and preach the gospel to all creation.'" He punctuated the passage with an extended silence.

My church belonged to the Christian Missionary Alliance, which prides itself on the number of missionaries sent worldwide, and evangelizing was a central component of our Youth Group. Sitting there surrounded by close friends and discussing such weighty topics as the eternal souls of the heathen and the return of the Messiah, I remember being giddy with the magnitude of our endeavor. Not only were we enthusiastically working to bring on the end of the world, we were operating under a heavenly mandate to do so.

Most people do find a titillating joy in contemplating the end of days. Apocalyptic fiction and end-of-the-world movies have always enjoyed a large fanbase, but actively striving for Armageddon remains the domain of Bond villains and religious fundamentalists. Buying up hours of late-night airtime on cable networks, the International Fellowship of Christians and Jews urges Evangelicals to open their wallets and pay for Jews to move to Israel. I first watched one of these infomercials back around 2004 and thought it a splendid idea. See, my church and thus my parents and thus myself had been swept up in the burgeoning tide of Christian Zionism. Today, the movement boasts millions of adherents, with the most powerful group being Christians United for Israel (CUFI), containing over 8 million members. The brainchild of televangelist John Hagee and the omnipresent Jerry Falwell, CUFI makes a name for itself by pushing ultra-right-wing Zionism on the international level. At first glance, a Jewish/Hagee alliance may seem an odd marriage. After all, Hagee is on the record as claiming that Hitler's bloodline consisted entirely of "accursed, genocidally murderous half-breed Jews." However, upon further inspection, the confusion dissipates. It's that LaHaye death cult all over again. Underlaying all other Christian Zionist motives are two beliefs. The first one was encapsulated by Vice President Mike Pence at the CUFI conference in 2019: "We stand with Israel because we cherish that ancient promise that those who bless her will be blessed." Mr Pence is referring to Numbers 24:9: "Whoever blesses Israel will be blessed, and whoever curses Israel will be cursed." It is hard to stress how strongly Evangelicals buy into this. My father counts it as the primary reason Trump got his vote in the 2020 election. The second belief is that every Jew (or at least a good portion of 'em?) must return to Israel before the second coming of Christ. Hence all the efforts by otherwise indifferent Evangelicals to help the chosen people find their way back to the promised land.

Christianity has never existed without a focus on the end times. That's kind of its thing. What hasn't always been its thing is a self-pitying demand for reactionary politics. Understanding the path Christianity took from a religion firmly rooted in radical pacifism and selflessness to trumpeting individualism, nationalism, and capitalism is complex to say the least. No matter how meandering the journey may have been, I believe there to be a point in history where that complex journey took its tightest bend in that direction.

On October 27, 312 CE, the Roman emperor Constantine had a vision of the cross with the words "in this sign, conquer" written in the sky above it. The next day, he had his troops paint the sign upon their shields before engaging in battle with his political rival Maxentius. Constantine killed Maxentius and went on to establish himself as the sole ruler of Rome. Constantine made Christianity a tool of the state, and the religion went from persecuted to persecutors. It has maintained that position to this day with only a few hiccups.

One such hiccup was liberation theology, as popularized

in the 1960s. Latin American bishops attempted to revive the Gospels with their focus on pacifism, community, and taking care of the poor. Liberation theology has been routinely stamped down by the policies and actions of the United States. Administration after administration and their Evangelical supporters actively pursued its eradication. When liberation theology's policy of "preferential treatment for the poor" began to spread across Latin America, the USA responded with out and out terrorism. The CIA instigated a coup in Brazil, setting up a fascist dictator after too many Brazilian politicians picked up the call of liberation. In the 1980s America trained Salvadoran special forces with the specific task of ridding the country of pesky Jesuits who refused to back down from their religious convictions. Needless to say, it was not a bloodless effort. The liberation movement was seriously stalled when soldiers, fresh out of training at Fort Bragg, stormed José Simeón Cañas Central American University and executed six Jesuit priests who were the movement's leading intellectuals. Let's just hope that if Jesus does make a reappearance on Earth, he keeps his mouth shut about equality, justice, and the poor.

As both a creed and a tool, Christianity has always found a home in American political and civil life. Coming from a monarchy where religion and government were thoroughly entwined, the framers knew how harmful religion could be in the hands of the state. They attempted to enshrine a few safeguards into our founding documents. Still, the country was deeply religious, and an intermingling was impossible to halt completely. Lately, there has been an effort to push a revisionist history of America. In this version of events, America was not simply populated by many religious people; it was founded entirely by Christians and shaped specifically by Evangelical precepts.

The mostly deist founders fought for the separation of church and state so diligently that even allowing chaplains in the military was thought of as an affront to the first amendment by the very man who wrote it, James Madison. He also disliked the day of prayer in the White House. George Washington would leave church before communion was taken because he believed, "To do otherwise would be an ostentatious display of religious zeal" inappropriate for his position. When confronted by a parishioner, he stopped going to church publicly altogether. Then there was Jefferson's Bible in which he had cut out any mention of the supernatural. Arguably the most respectable of the founding fathers and by far the staunchest proponent of democracy, Thomas Paine, spoke to the topic in *The Age of Reason* where he said:

The only religion that has not been invented, and that has in it every evidence of divine originality, is pure and simple deism. It must have been the first and will probably be the last that man believes. But pure and simple deism does not answer the purpose of despotic governments. They cannot lay hold of religion as an engine but by mixing it with human inventions, and making their own authority a part; neither does it answer the avarice of priests, but by incorporating themselves and their functions with it, and becoming, like the government, a party in the system. It is this which forms the otherwise mysterious connection of Church and State; the Church humane, and the State tyrannic.

Benjamin Franklin and Ethan Allen disdained the idea of religion intermingling with government in any way whatsoever, and each wrote extensively on its poisoning effect. Franklin's personal creed was that of a diest who believed good works in this life mattered most. He stopped attending his Presbyterian church after he began to feel morality had taken a backseat to dogma. A few months before his death in 1790, Franklin responded to a letter from the President of Yale, Ezra Stiles, in which he wrote:

As to Jesus of Nazareth, my Opinion of whom you particularly desire, I think the System of Morals and his Religion as he left them to us, the best the World ever saw, or is likely to see; but I apprehend it has received various corrupting Changes, and I have with most of the present Dissenters in England, some Doubts as to his Divinity: tho' it is a Question I do not dogmatise upon – I see no harm however in its being believed, if that Belief has the good Consequence as probably it has, of making his Doctrines more respected and better observed, especially as I do not perceive that the Supreme takes it amiss, by distinguishing the Believers, in his Government of the World, with any particular Marks of his Displeasure.

The Treaty of Tripoli, penned by John Adams in 1796, expresses quite plainly the object of the last few paragraphs: "the Government of the United States of America is not, in any sense, founded on the Christian religion." It has been argued that this clause was only added to appease the Muslims of the Barbary coast, thus ensuring safe passage for American ships in the Mediterranean. To that I say, unquestionably it was, but does Jesus need to be disowned two more times before a cock crows for the rather unchristian pragmatism to shine through?

Even with the founders' efforts, the separation of church and state in America has always been tenuous at best. A precarious balance was only made possible by the sheer multitude of religious beliefs. Christianity was by far the most prevalent religion, but each denomination within it feared the ambitions of the others. In fact, it was the disenfranchisement of the Danbury Baptists at the hands of the Congregationalists, who had recently been established as Connecticut's state denomination, that first inspired the phrase so often thought to be in the constitution.

President Jefferson responded to a plea for support from the Baptist leadership by saying:

> Believing with you that religion is a matter which lies solely between man and his God, that he owes account to none other for his faith or his worship, that the legislative powers of government reach actions only, and not opinions, I contemplate with sovereign reverence that act of the whole American people which declared that their legislature would "make no law respecting an establishment of religion, or prohibiting the free exercise thereof," thus building a wall of separation between Church and State.

That wall, already in disrepair, would find itself besieged like never before during the American Civil War.

Chapter 5

The Civil War

Religion is an insult to human dignity. With or without it you would have good people doing good things and evil people doing evil things. But for good people to do evil things, that takes religion.
Steven Weinberg, Nobel Laureate

A few years back, I visited the Stone mountain monolith outside of Atlanta. A kindly park volunteer took a moment to inform me that the entirety of the edifice was larger than a football field and bigger than Mount Rushmore. He spoke that second bit of information with evident pride. Beaming as if he had defaced the mountainside by carving the effigies of Jefferson Davis, Robert E. Lee, and Stonewall Jackson himself. Another park visitor had stopped to hear what knowledge was being doled out. The interloper resembled nothing so much as a mall Santa in overalls. "Won't be long now before they come and tear the whole damn thing down." The mall Santa followed his statement with an honest-to-god spit of chewing tobacco. Atlanta, while in the south, does not truly belong to the capital "S" South, so this caricature of the Southern hillbilly felt more like a poorly done Hollywood recreation than the flesh and bone be-whiskered man standing directly beside me. Even in Atlanta, Southern pride is very much a thing. Drive any direction out of the city, and it becomes a way of life.

To some prideful citizens of the 11 states that once made up the doomed nation, the Confederacy represents a certain wholesomeness, a specific order where everyone knew their position, a place not unlike medieval England. In fact, slavery was instituted in an effort to recreate the old-world aristocracy. And like an even shittier Medieval Times, the present-day South tries to reanimate the days of yore. Complete with year-round Civil War reenactments, erecting statue after statue, and living out a good 'ol homespun racism.

In many minds, The Confederacy stands for a time when God's providence was known and clearly understood. To hear them talk about it, the Civil War had almost nothing to do with slavery at all. To this day, many private schools below the Mason Dixon refuse to even call it the "Civil War," instead preferring the title "The War of Northern Aggression." So what, pray tell, do these modern-day butternuts believe the Civil War was all about? Turns out it's pretty simple. The Southern understanding, then and now, frames the conflict as rugged individualism vs. a tyrannical state. The "fighting chaplain" Isaac Tichenor gave this revelatory sermon on the roots of the Civil War to a group of Confederate soldiers in 1863, during one of the federally mandated days of fasting:

> If God governs the world, then his hand is in this war in which we are engaged. It matters not that the wickedness of man brought it upon us, that it was caused by the mad attempts of fanaticism to deprive us of our rights, overthrow our institutions, and impose upon us a yoke which, as freemen, we had resolved never to bear.

The wickedness he is referencing ain't slavery. To Tichenor and his compatriots, the real wickedness rested squarely on the shoulders of the Northern aggressors. State's rights bitches! What's more, bemoaning the imposition of a hypothetical yoke while imposing an actual yoke on over 4 million people speaks to a lack of self-awareness that didn't die with Tichenor.

Fittingly, the bloodiest war in American history remains its most contentious. While some claim the impetus of state's rights, an equally unsatisfactory explanation is given by others. Something like, "The evil of Southern slavery finally became too much for the morally superior North to endure." However, both of these explanations are lacking. If it was solely a state's rights issue, how could the wholesale slaughter of yesterday's brethren be warranted? If the unjust treatment of black men, women, and children was so close to the Union's heart, why then was the North so accommodating to Southern slave owners before the war? "Let as many servants as are under the yoke count their own masters worthy of all honour, that the name of God and his doctrine be not blasphemed." 2 Timothy 6:1

Frederick Douglass wrote in his autobiography, *Narrative of the Life of Frederick Douglass, An American Slave,* that when his master converted to Methodism, he only became crueler. Douglass had hoped that his master's new religious convictions would result in freedom for the families he held under the whip; instead, it only provided divine justification for his barbarity.

Before America was torn in two by war, it experienced a religious mitosis of sorts. Churches littered the landscape of both the North and the South, all belonging to the same denominations. The three largest confessional groups at the time were the Presbyterians, the Baptists, and the Methodists. Each split on the topic of slavery, but more importantly, on what *God* thought of slavery.

Southern ministers pointed out that it mattered little what one's personal convictions were, only what God said. They had chapter and verse at their fingertips. After all, Paul himself sent the escaped slave Onesimus back to his master, and of all the things Jesus spoke against, he remained silent on the topic of slavery. The Old Testament is awash with instructions on how to treat slaves, gentile and Hebrew alike. Rev Ben Palmer summed up the Southern attitude toward slavery in his November 29, 1860 sermon, "The South has a divine obligation to conserve and to perpetuate the institution of domestic slavery as now existing...We will stand by our trust: and God be with the right!"

The Northern clergymen had a more nuanced, yet they

argued, a more biblically sound approach. The nature of Jesus' teaching could not possibly allow for the institution of slavery. Looking back into the Presbyterian church, who thankfully did an excellent job at keeping the minutes for their meetings, we can see how even in 1818, they felt the institution of slavery violated God's word:

> We consider the voluntary enslaving of one portion of the human race by another, as a gross violation of the most precious and sacred rights of human nature; as utterly inconsistent with the law of God, which requires us to love our neighbors as ourselves, and as totally irreconcilable with the principles and spirit of the gospel of Christ which enjoin that all things whatsoever ye would that men should do to you, do ye even so to them.

Northern and Southern churches claimed divine providence and preached hellfire from the pulpit with absolute certainty. Carrying on the tradition of Whitefield and Edwards, a wave of "millennial nationalism" swept across the North and South. Each believed they were establishing the preliminary societies necessary for Christ's return as prescribed in the books of Daniel and Revelation. A thousand years of paradise prior to God's final judgment of mankind. Southern ministers saw their plight as parallel to Israel of old and would quote scripture accordingly. Rev W.T. Hamilton argued in his treatise *Domestic Servitude As Sanctioned By the Bible* that:

> Were Abraham now living among us, with all his slaves around him, sealed though they were in God's own covenant by divine command, he would, by modern abolitionists, be excluded from the church, as a cruel, selfish, hard-hearted man, a bloodyhanded man-stealer.

Whether or not they supported slavery became less of an issue in the face of whether or not they supported the kingdom of God. Hamilton's statement does ring quietly of self-awareness. Yes, if Abraham lived outside of the Middle East at pretty much any point in history, past his own, he would absolutely be considered a monster. "Hey kiddo, yeah so...uh, a voice told me to murder you on top this mountain. Yeah, it was the same voice that told me to cut all the tips off everyone's dicks...So what? I don't see your point."

The wall that separated church from state was only as strong as those willing to uphold it. Religious tensions kept pace with the abolitionist movement. A movement of which Lincoln was not an avid supporter. Politically you could be on either side of the religious divide; you could not be religiously ambivalent. In the face of this new reality, Lincoln, who never belonged to any church and only proclaimed the most nebulous of faiths, was forced to cave to the pressures of an impassioned electorate to win his seat in the 1847 Congress by saying:

I have never denied the truth of the Scriptures; and I have never spoken with intentional disrespect of religion in general, or of any denomination of Christians in particular – I do not think I could myself, be brought to support a man for office, whom I knew to be an open enemy of, and scoffer at, religion.

Honest Abe may not have told a lie, but empty political jargon was not outside his moral objections. When war did break out in 1861, the conflict itself was oft seen as a punishment for sins, both personal and cultural. Union preachers fed absolute moral certitude to their congregants. They would claim the Union was God's chosen nation predestined to triumph. The sin of slavery was one thing, but the evil of succession made Southerners into apostates. Not all abolitionists attacked slavery on purely religious grounds. William Loyd Garrison wrote in his abolitionist paper *The Liberator* that, "if a good case could be made in scripture for slavery then to hell with the Bible!" Unfortunately, men like Garrison were the outliers. Many abolitionists wanted to end slavery then deport all the freed slaves back to Africa. Or would only work toward ending slavery but would not personally associate with any black people whatsoever.

When the Union was routed in the war's first battle at Bull's Run, it was seen in the North as evidence that the nation was not yet godly enough. Shortly after the battle, Northern minister Horace Bushnell preached that the loss to the Confederacy was a direct result of the Union being a godless nation. He urged his congregants to turn away from the constitution and toward a more divine form of government. He opined that where it should be "In the beginning, God" the Union accepted "In the beginning, Thomas Jefferson." It's almost refreshing to hear a Christian nationalist vilify the founding fathers. And a Christian nationalist he was. As with the majority of Northern pastors, Bushnell claimed that when the Union defeated the South, America would finally become "God's own nation."

Bushnell's low opinion of the founding documents was shared by the new Confederacy, along with his Christian nationalism. Upon secession, the South wrote up a flurry of their own founding papers. For the most part, they were mirror images of the Union's; however, there were some notable differences. For example, here is the preamble to the Confederate Constitution:

> We, the people of the Confederate States, each state acting in its sovereign and independent character, in order to form a permanent federal government, establish justice, insure domestic tranquillity, and secure the blessings of liberty to ourselves and our posterity – invoking the favor and

guidance of Almighty God – do ordain and establish this Constitution for the Confederate States of America.

The Confederacy sought to rectify the godless nature of the founding documents by invoking God in almost every one of their important papers. In so doing, they were assured by their clergymen to attain and retain God's favor.

Not to be outdone by the Confederacy, a powerful assembly of Northern clergymen formed the National Reform Association and attempted to push a constitutional amendment that would not merely declare America to be a Christian nation but would mention Jesus by name in the preamble. Surely this would finally nail down the wiley grace of God for the Union. The motion eventually failed, but always the statesman, Lincoln compromised and allowed for "In God We Trust" to be printed on newly minted two cent pieces.

As the war progressed, each side attributed their losses to sin and their gains to providence. The chaplaincy was expanded dramatically, and religious revivals swept through Union and Confederate camps quicker than dysentery. Both Lincoln and Davis would call for days of "prayer and humiliation" after lost battles. The idea that God's hand was directing everything from weather patterns to troop movements was pervasive throughout the war.

Slavery was important to the Northern economy and absolutely essential to the Southern economy; not to mention, pivotal to the very framework of their society. The political control of that system is a root cause of the Civil War. Economics demanded slavery, but religious absolutism allowed for a wholesale slaughter that was previously unthinkable. Nations and armies fighting for nothing more than boundaries, borders, and political rationales know when to cut their losses. A military fighting with divine mandate makes no provision for failure. The Confederacy continued to fight long after any real chance of success had died. To do otherwise demanded a very uncomfortable confrontation with providence. How could God turn his back on a holy nation? They could not have been wrong about slavery the entire time, could they? Certainly not! The Bible supported slavery, but the Southern slave owners had fallen short of biblical standards for the treatment of slaves. Or so claimed Southern Reformers. These Reformers promised that if slave owners were to conform to biblical criteria, God's favor would be again on their side. These reforms got nowhere. The war continued, and the bloodshed only worsened.

The Union was facing its own inner struggles. The war was supposed to have been a short campaign. Why had God allowed for such butchery to take place if it had been his will from the beginning that the North should prevail? Questions like this were strongly felt in Lincoln's second inaugural speech:

> Each looked for an easier triumph and a result less fundamental and astounding. Both read the same Bible and pray to the same God and each invokes His aid against the other. It may seem strange that any men should dare to ask a just God's assistance in wringing their bread from the sweat of other men's faces but let us judge not that we be not judged. The prayers of both could not be answered – that of neither has been answered fully. The Almighty has His own purposes.

Religious zeal waxed and waned throughout the war. Chaplains saw their pay cut, soldiers drank, gambled, and swore, while revivals saw hundreds of converts. Men dying on the battlefield both cursed God and rejoiced in their salvation. By the war's end, questions concerning providence and divine mandate and even manifest destiny began to feel rather silly. Far from rejecting their civil religion, the majority of the reunited country found solace in a more nominal form of religious expression. The Civil War had laid waste to much of the country and killed over 2.5

percent of the population, but it had also destroyed a growing religious absolutism. Not for some time would preachers or politicians be able to make grand claims of God's providence or arrogate for themselves God's favor and still be taken seriously.

The explosive popularity of national millennialism before the war was also forced into retreat. But like I said, the end of the world is kind of Christianity's bread and butter. A new interpretation of biblical events was burrowing its roots into the blood-soaked soil. Premillennial Dispensationalism, without getting too deep into the theological bushes, this interpretation had a whole lot more that needed to take place on Earth before Christ's 1000-year reign could begin. Remember the *Left Behind* series? Dispensationalists believe God interacts with humanity differently at different times throughout history. A handy way of explaining why the God of the Old Testament was pretty gung-ho for genocide, infanticide, and all-around nastiness while the God of the New Testament seems a bit more cuddly. It can also rationalize why the sick are no longer miraculously healed or the dead raised from the grave. One of the most critical aspects of Dispensationalism is that it can be treated as a literal roadmap to future events. Albeit a rather "hindsight is 20/20" kind of roadmap.

The eventual intermerging of viewpoints after the war resulted in a hodgepodge of beliefs within Evangelicalism. As with the nation as a whole, churches from both sides wanted to put the whole affair behind them. In the name of unity and church seemliness, accountability was replaced by a more accommodating and tepid centerline. On a national level, this could be seen as well. Other than a brief stint in jail for Jefferson Davis, men like Robert E. Lee, Davis, and Robert A. Toombs were never asked to give an account for their actions or face any real form of justice.

Every Christian school I ever attended used the same Abeka curriculum. Formerly known as A Beka Book Publishing, Abeka is affiliated with Pensacola Christian College and caters to an Evangelical audience. Not much of a problem when math is being taught, but a much bigger problem when instructing in, let's say, the history of the Civil War? In their 2015 "history" book entitled *America: Land I Love,* slavery is dramatically downplayed as central to the war and described as merely "a likely causal factor"; it also proposes the war may have been sent as a punishment from God for America's "religious apostasy and cultism." Why this revisionist history instead of some other equally ahistorical account? Abeka kindly answers that question too, albeit unintentionally. "After the war, the South suffered, but it rose from the ashes to become the Bible Belt, a part of the country that has continued to stand firm on the fundamentals of Christian faith."

Chapter 6

Back to Panama

Growing up in the Deep South meant growing up in a culture inextricable from Evangelicalism regardless of whether or not you attended Church. Attending a white flight school under the auspices of a "Christian education" certainly amplified the influence. I didn't grow up reading the fundamentalist books, wearing a purity ring, or attending purity balls like many of my acquaintances. Still, the atmosphere was so thick with Evangelical gender expectations that I couldn't help but internalize, distress over, and worst of all, exemplify them.

As a result, I was sought after by the men and boys around me who had been taught that meekness, modesty, and agreeability were the highest qualities in a woman. I attended a Christian college and was proposed to four times before my 21st birthday. Only one of the suitors and I went on a date prior to these proposals. "Ring by Spring" was not taken lightly on campus. "Courtship" seemed to regularly be on offer, an obviously more godly alternative to dating, which was considered "practice for divorce." My chemistry teacher's assistant professed his love for me in the pouring rain after my first tutoring session. The poor guy was drenched while standing only a few feet from shelter because he was not allowed any closer to the girls' dorm. I had no indication of his feelings for me before this awkward confession. The head resident advisor blithely informed me that my name had come up more than once at the last male RA meeting in response to the obviously normal game of "if you had to marry someone right now, who would it be." I could go on.

This may all sound like the experiences of a spoiled high school hot girl, but I was neither hot nor spoiled by the unwanted attention. Having been taught that I was responsible for both the actions and thoughts of my male counterparts since before I can remember, I felt the full weight of my responsibility. It was a psychologically tumultuous time to say the least. On two separate occasions by the age of 15, two boys threatened to kill themselves while holding weapons if I did not agree to date them.

After each bewildering encounter, I was certain I had done something wrong and felt immense guilt as I apologized to them profusely. I realize now, each of these interactions were designed to make me feel guilty or inferior in order to obtain my submission. Attempts that I'm ashamed to admit were frequently successful.

Kate, Illinois

In 1995 my parents were working at the mission "Bootcamp" where my mother was a secretary and my father was in the video productions department. Yes, my legally blind father was in video productions. We received word that with the ousting of Noriega, all history of my father's deportation had been lost. We returned to Panama that year. Instead of working in remote jungles, my parents were assigned to a boarding school the mission ran in the small town of Chame. They took up the position of dorm parents with around 12 children in their care. Much later, the dormitories and the school would undergo an investigation after dozens of abuse accusations had surfaced. My parents were never implicated.

One of the mission's mottos was "God can use anybody," and the leadership really took it to heart. People who had no business being around children were given positions of authority. The mission's strict fundamentalist Evangelical views empowered abusers with the mandate of heaven. A pervasive belief existed among the missionaries that the good Lord would never allow for such people to worm their way into the presence of the godly undetected.

Only the training and education administered by the leadership was viewed as having any value. The mission offered little to no training on spotting abuse. They didn't have classes on child development or child psychology. Even mandatory reporting was deemed unnecessary if the abuse happened abroad. Detection of abuse relied almost entirely on the victims speaking out. The atmosphere created by the mission ensured that speaking out about anything would be ill-received.

Disturbances on the mission field were often attributed to Satan attempting to derail God's work. Thus, accusations could be dismissed as nothing more than flaming arrows of the Devil to be sidestepped in achieving a much larger divine plan. Corporal punishment was not only regularly utilized; it was encouraged as biblical doctrine. I was not a victim of abuse and told as much to the investigators who interviewed me in 2010, but I was often on the receiving end of my third-grade teacher's ping-pong paddle. She was an ancient old woman with a shaky swing and a propensity to fall asleep during class. Her paddlings were more a source of after school jokes than a form of correction.

It is no wonder that schools operated by this mission across the globe have come under investigation with 59 perpetrators identified and hundreds of victims. These victims suffered rape, sexual abuse, beatings, and mental abuse at the hands of men and women tasked with their protection. The environment created by the mission fostered abuse and helped to justify covering it up for years. Victims were told to pray and stay silent or risk ruining the all-important ministries of their abusers. In 1992, investigators got ahold of a field memo from the mission in Senegal that outlines how to respond to an accusation of sexual abuse.

If it is a homosexual act with a child, the person will be dismissed immediately and may never be considered for membership in the mission again. If it is a heterosexual act the person will be dismissed immediately but could be considered for ministry again in the future depending on the case. If it occurs in the field, it is not necessary to report it to the Senegalese or US authorities.

Clearly, the priority is placed on the perpetrator, not the victim. Attempting to distance themselves from their sordid history, New Tribes Mission (NTM) rebranded themselves Ethnos 360 in 2017. They are currently back in hot water for attempting to reach uncontacted tribes in the Amazon during a pandemic. Given the isolated nature of these groups and the deadliness of Covid, this evangelism could result in genocide.

NTM believes in the imminent return of Jesus to Earth and that all who died without accepting him as their personal savior will spend eternity in hell. Imagine being a member of the Yanomami, Nukak, or Embera people when a white man shows up with unimaginable medicines and technologies. He cures your sick and gives you tools that make your life immeasurably easier. Next, he tells you that he has with him the one true message of God, and without it, you and your family will burn forever in darkness. You would have to be a fool to ignore his revelation. The understandable elation of salvation from a previously unknown danger is followed by the gradual realization that every single one of your deceased loved ones is currently being tortured and will be for eternity. An actual recording exists of the precise moment celebration turns to the deepest conceivable lament for the Mouk people of Papua New Guinea.

NTM used the footage in a missionary recruitment video entitled "Ee-Taow." In the video, missionary Mark Zook goes step by step through the conversion process. Starting with the book of Genesis, where the creation myth of Adam and Eve is taught as both literal and indisputable. It then moves through every major Old Testament story until the crucifixion and subsequent resurrection of Christ. Importantly they take time to "debunk" evolution along the way. In Ee-Taow, NTM exploits the genuine sorrow of the Mouk tribe as a recruitment tool.

The souls of unimaginable multitudes are at risk if you do not commit your life to the mission right now!

However, the mass conversion of the Mouk may not be all that it appears. Unfortunately, there is precious little information available on the Mouk people outside of the NTM blogosphere. To get a more complete picture of who the Mouk were, I reached out to anthropologist Andrew Lattas, who has worked extensively in the bush Kaliai region, the home of the Mouk people. He informed me that the Mouk were far from the uncontacted animistic tribe that NTM had portrayed. Catholic missionaries had long since left their mark on New Britain, and the majority of the Mouk had previously converted to Catholicism.

The Mouk had their own mythology stemming from WWII cargo cults that incorporated Christianity and which featured the imminent return of a local deity, called Titikolo. In local myths, he is often identified as a black Christ, who had left for America years before and whose return the American missionaries seemed to foretell. Professor Lattas wrote a fascinating book about the people in the region entitled *Cultures of Secrecy: Reinventing Race in Bush Kaliai Cargo Cults*. He also wrote a specific article in the sixty-sixth volume of *Oceania* entitled, "Memory, Forgetting and the New Tribes Mission in West New Britain." In this article he tells of a much more manipulative NTM introducing Evangelicalism into the area. He refers to the NTM missionary as "Sign."

...the new missionaries asked Mouk big men to come and tell their stories. Those who went gave Sign the story of the trickster god Titikolo, who is known for changing his name as he visits different communities. I was told how, when Mouk storytellers recited Titikolo's different names, Sign opened up his copy of the Bible and replied that these names could all be found in its pages. Paul, the son of one of these respected storytellers, gave me his father's account of this meeting: "They [Mouk storytellers] told the story, and Sign said that all these names are here in the book [Bible]. [Sign speaking:] This story is true, the names of this man are here."...In 1986 another storyteller, Nangile, told me that Sign informed these storytellers that one name was missing from their story, and if they could provide this name, the new law would come.

When I corresponded with Professor Lattas about the Mouk conversion, he told me, "local cargo cult beliefs were exploited to produce the conversions. The account by the NTM of that conversion is misleading and a sanitized version of why people converted from Catholicism to the Evangelical faith...NTM exploited that local culture whilst presenting it as straightforward religious conversion." That's not to say the conversion was not heartfelt on the behalf of the Mouk. Apparently, the Catholics had not pushed the concept of hell quite as fervently as NTM had. The NTM influence in the region resulted in what was essentially a new cargo cult. Blending traditional beliefs and Evangelicalism with the personal emanation of specific NTM missionaries, many locals would come to describe themselves as followers of the New Tribes Mission before they might call themselves followers of Christ.

But I digress. My family arrived back on the mission field of Panama in 1995. NTM expected each missionary to raise their own funds and my parents were a bit behind. Our first year back was not one of absolute deprivation, but spam was regularly featured on the dinner plate, as were sardines and copious amounts of rice, all to be washed down with chalky powdered milk. Occasionally there would be a sigh of relief from around the table when we saw chicken was on the menu. It wasn't until a year later that beef would appear. Isn't it odd how we remember things? I am sure that my use of food as a metric of the first year says something about me. Recitation from dusty, tape-bound books containing the exploits of long-dead Protestant missionaries in the Orient or Africa was once the preferred method for endowing students with moral fortitude and spiritual courage. The popular routine disappeared from American public schools more than a few generations ago. However, like corporal punishment and an Urkelesque approach to style, the practice had a steadfast home at my boarding school in Chame. Invariably, my wizened and often flatulent fourth-grade teacher, Mrs Woodhead, would doze off in the middle of reading some passage about Hudson Taylor or David Livingston. Equally as often, and to the consternation of the rest of the class, a schoolmate, whom I shall not name as to graciously spare him some well-earned embarrassment, would wake her mid-snore and assist in regaining our place in the story. My science class featured artistic renditions of dinosaurs roaming around with their human caretakers. Memorization of the Bible was required in every grade. Mrs Woodhead put it like this, "We memorize scripture so that whenever something happens, anything at all, we won't even have to think, and the perfect Bible verse will 'poof' come to mind!" I remember even then thinking how much I disliked people who routinely quoted scripture.

The school's primary function was to imprint fundamentalist ideology onto malleable minds. With little framework for which to contextualize my situation, the authoritarian and pharisaical aether that governed everything from what I was allowed to read to who I was allowed to befriend all went unremarked. Still, I found myself testing the currents of this straight and narrow river. Like a small child in any swift current, I offered little resistance before being swept under. That isn't to say I didn't thoroughly enjoy this period in my life. I regularly look back with sappy nostalgia. Similar to Wisconsin, the growing theological and ideological cage was offset by an almost negligent amount of freedom to explore.

One particularly favored spot was a wide and stony river about 6 miles from the school. This place, perhaps more than any other single location, was formative to my childhood identity. Entire days were spent exploring its bends and whirlpools. Populated by snakes, caiman, a variety of fish and crustaceans, the river served as watering grounds for herds of cows and horses as well as a hunting ground for storks, lizards, and the occasional margay. The skies above the water were alive with parrots and toucans. This sanctuary fed the wildlife and my imagination in equal strides. It was impossible not to have a sense of adventure in this place. Merely getting there took a trek through cow pastures, along steep ravines, and into dense jungle. My best friend and I would fish with small explosives and "hunt" caiman along the river banks. We had never killed one but caught and released several footlong babies over the years. One day of exploration in particular is worth referencing here as it provided a poignant metaphor later in life.

The dull clicking sound of air suddenly being released from my Daisy pellet gun signaled the end of our hour-long pursuit. I had become quite the shot since my tenth birthday, and the proof was flopping helplessly on the ground a few meters away. Evan and I dashed over to where the bird lay dying, pumping the air rifle as I ran. The enormous crow was dead before we reached it. "Quick, cut off the head before the blood dries up!" Evan said after a short pause to admire my marksmanship. "You do it," I replied, handing him my pocket knife. Without hesitation, he took the knife, cut a slit at the base of the neck, and drained about an ounce of blood into a small Tupperware container. "You think it'll be enough?" I asked. "I don't know, don't think they're like sharks or anything, but it can't hurt," Evan surmised. With the dead bird, container of blood, and three spears made of nail-topped broomsticks in tow, we headed for the bike shed. This would be the day we finally killed a croc.

Transporting the long spears proved to be rather cumbersome on my ten-speed Huffy, but I managed. We did run into a bit of trouble when crossing one of the several cow pastures on the way to the river. We knew this paddock was the home of an incredibly territorial Brahman bull. We had had multiple run-ins with him before, none of which had been pleasant. "You have to take one of these," I said, tossing Evan a spear. "I'll never outrun him if he comes for us," I continued. The bull was on the far side of the field, eying us warily. It was probably my imagination, but I could hear the depth of his breathing increase. Evan caught the spear as effortlessly as he did everything and stood on his pedals ready to push off. The spear was now lying across his handlebars, as were the other two on mine. "You ready?" he whispered, and without waiting for my answer, he launched forward across the pasture. We only needed to get to a gate about 100 yards diagonal from where we were, but that 100 yards stretched out into miles when I noticed the massive white bull barreling full canter in our direction. His horns lowered to the ground and my legs burned as I pushed harder and harder on the pedals. Evan was already squeezing through the gap in the barbed wire when I realized I was not going to make it before the bull reached me. Leaping from my bike, I threw the two remaining spears over the fence and dove through the narrow gate. The bicycle worked as a decoy, drawing the bull's ire and received a bit of a thrashing. The big guy soon lost interest and sauntered back to his shady corner, proud of his day's work. The bike's chain had come off, and the seat sported a new tear, but overall it was not much worse for wear, and we continued on to the river.

A short walk down the bank was an enclave of water unaffected by the river's currents. We knew it to be where the caiman usually congregated. Sure enough, there were 20 or maybe 30 sets of yellow eyes floating above the surface. The U-shaped pocket of water curved away from the river's main body and into the trees. The bank was thick mud and brush. One old dying tree, more prominent and closer to the river's edge than the others, had thick branches jutting out over the water.

Evan slung his backpack to the ground and pulled out a

plastic bag with a dead bird in it, the container of blood, and some string we had brought from home. The plan was to tie the bird by the feet then toss him out into the center of the caiman. We'd quickly pull it back to shore, hopefully being followed by a hungry reptile. When the caiman opened its jaws expecting an avine lunch, it would receive 6 inches of cold steel down its throat. Foolproof. That these caimans were often 5 or 6 feet long and around 100lbs of armor-clad muscle meant nothing to us. Under 100 pounds myself, the weight of my ambition more than made up the difference.

Having missed the mark twice already I handed the dangling bird to Evan. "Give it a try," I said without a hint of defeat in my voice. Evan took the soaked corpse and started twirling it by the string. He released his grip at the apex of the arch, and the bird flew once more skywards. Much higher than my previous tosses. So much higher in fact that the crow became tangled in the branches of one tall tree overhanging the water. Evan and I looked at each other, and a new plan came together in both our minds at the same time. "The angle is all wrong down here. Best we could do is stab them in the tongue and make it mad," Evan said reasonably. "Yeah, but from up on that branch, we could get right down his throat!" I replied with building excitement.

Perched on a branch about 4 feet above the water and with dozens of circling crocodiles below, we readied ourselves for the killing blow. Evan had remembered the jar of blood and emptied it into the murky brown water beneath us. I was a bit further out on the branch and was tasked with dipping the dead crow in and out of the water. Evan, a foot or two closer to shore, held a spear ready with both hands. The plan appeared to be working. The caimans shifted their snouts toward the commotion. One in particular separated itself from the float and slowly made its way to the dangling bird.

"Hey, this branch seems a little dead." Evan's voice snapped the tension. The comment felt so out of place when we were on the precipice of executing a plan we had spent the entirety of our shared boyhood putting together. I began to ask what on earth he was talking about when I was interrupted by a sudden cracking sound and Evan rising up into the sky on a broken branch. I hit the water, still straddling my end of the branch. Immediately the nearest crocodiles shot under the water and my feet plunged into the sucking mud at the bottom of the river. The water was not deep and my face was only inches below the surface. The silt in the water stung my eyes as I peered up at my best friend shouting down at me. The water between us muted whatever he was saying, but I could see him gesticulating in the direction where the curious caiman had been. Pulling one foot out of its shoe then the other, I was able to free myself from the mud and shoot to the surface. No sooner had air filled my lungs then I searched wildly around me for gaping jaws and amber eyes. No open mouths but there were eyes, so many eyes and getting closer. I could now hear Evan shouting, "Throw it! Throw it!" over and over again. Somehow in the fall, I had managed to grab hold of the dead crow and was now holding it above my head. Incredibly, I was filled with reluctance to throw away the object of so much labor. A sentiment that persisted even after spotting multiple sets of approaching eyes. Finally, I tossed the bird at the nearest of the caimans. Here is where my memory may not be entirely trustworthy because I swear that I saw multiple caimans jump out of the water, snapping at the bird in a cartoonish flurry. Evan's shout had now changed to "Swim! Swim!" I submerged myself once more to push off against that oh so treacherous branch. Shooting forward, I swam faster than my scrawny limbs should have been capable of doing. I reached the shore, coughing and sputtering but miraculously intact.

This story has served me well over the last few years. I use it as an interesting ice breaker in the first weeks of class when my students are still deciding if I'm too old to be relatable. It was also a hit on dates and at parties. Strangely enough, after nearly finding myself filling the stomachs of a dozen hungry crocodiles, I stopped thinking about the event almost entirely. It would be another 10 years before the memory came back to me while I sat huddled close to a fire on a remote New Zealand beach.

Even with hungry crocodiles and stringent religiosity, my life in Panama was an idyllic one. But, I do recall a sense that there was something profoundly wrong. Not necessarily with the sanctimonious preaching, but in the certitude of belief and the closed-off otherness in which we were required to dress ourselves. There were a litany of rules detailing appropriate interactions with "the locals." We were not allowed to hang out with them like we were allowed to hang out with members of the mission. All contact was strictly monitored and supervised. I can now understand that some of those rules were to protect callow, monastic youth from potential exploitation at the hands of the more experienced and savvy kids in the neighborhood. But still, the "us" and "them" juxtaposition developed a subconscious racial bias. A bias which many of us missionary kids continue to hold on to.

The school campus on which we lived existed in its own ecosystem. Holidays like Halloween were renamed and reinvented to be more "Christian." Many movies which debuted after 1960 were expunged from our lives, but not all of them. Surprisingly, I was allowed to watch quite a few violent movies like *Air Force One* with Harrison Ford and even a version of Mel Gibson's *Braveheart* where the single sex scene had been removed. It took me some time to sort out how the movies we were allowed to watch were chosen. Essentially it came down to a form of male chauvinism. Violence was okay, sensuality was not. Anything with strong male leads who rescued women but did not fuck them was okay. Kissing was acceptable, but not too much. An Indiana Jones amount of kissing, let's say. Anything where a father was portrayed as an idiot was banned. Which was an annoying trope in the 90s. Too strong of a woman lead? Questionable. Anything with new-age magic was not allowed, but if that magic was set in outer space and called the "force?" Then it was okay.

As a missionary kid, or MK for short, living on the mission field in 1998, many of the idiosyncrasies of Evangelical youth culture were drastically magnified. We had our own version of church, the culture wars, and even Youth Group. Every year during Shrovetide the MK Youth Group would join with the local Panamanian Youth Groups to ensconce ourselves high up in the crater of a dormant volcano to wait out the evils of Carnival. The crater had long since filled with ice cold rain water, giving the spot its name of La Laguna. Each time we sequestered ourselves there we would attempt to measure how deep the little lake was. Upon my last visit our 300 feet of rope still could not reach the nethermost depths. It was during this final visit to La Laguna that I assisted in an apparent exorcism.

At 11 I was too young to be a member of our Youth Group or to attend exorcisms, but my parents were supervising the retreat so I was invited along. The MK Youth Group numbered in the low teens but there were nearly 50 kids there in total. La Laguna provided an opportunity for many local kids to invite their otherwise non-churchgoing friends to an evangelizing event. One such invitee showed up with the Devil in him. While waiting in line for some horchata, this poor kid who I'll call Tomas was approached by one of the Panamanian youth leaders we'll call Pedro. Pedro introduced himself and pleasantly engaged in a bit of small talk. The conversation took a slight turn when Pedro noticed that Tomas was wearing a curious pendant around his neck. Upon closer inspection, Pedro came to the conclusion that the pendant was more than it appeared. He quickly informed Tomas that the necklace he wore was no ordinary bobble but was in fact a witch-doctor's totem. Tomas denied the claim amiably enough, insisting it was a gift from a friend and nothing more. Not to be thwarted in his endeavor to rid the horchata line of evil, Pedro insisted the charm be surrendered into his custody for destruction. Tomas did not take kindly to the youth leader's demeanor and grew more and more angry with each subsequent demand. Pedro eventually enlisted several male Youth Group attendees to assist in his holy crusade.

Tomas put up a spirited fight; punching, scratching, and shouting. I couldn't understand what he was yelling, his voice was already hoarse and I spoke embarrassingly little Spanish. As heroic of a defense as it was, he couldn't resist the five burly assailants for long. They plucked the amulet from its chain and smashed it under a rock. With each man to an appendage, Tomas was pinned to the ground while Pedro shouted "En el nombre de Jesucristo!" over and over again. Still unwilling to be subdued, he continued to buck and writhe. I was corralled with the rest of the camp into a small field only a few yards from the commotion. Forming a circle we stood there hand in hand, creepily singing hymns until Tomas, fatigued, eventually passed out. "Did you see him throw those guys like they were nothing?" "Yeah! One of 'em was tossed like, 20 feet away…it was so scary."

"Could you understand what he was saying?"

"No, he was speaking like five different languages, and his voice! I heard him talking before and that wasn't what he sounded like then."

The tale which almost immediately sprung from this sorry misadventure became one of brave Christian men exorcizing a demon and saving a soul. I witnessed the events and saw no sign of superhuman strength or a demonic polyglot, but that did not stop me from reporting that I had. The entirety of the camp was of one mind, there had been an exorcism and we had all helped cast out a demon with nothing more than our prayers and supplication. None of us were complicit in the assault of a teenager, we were doing the Lord's work.

Every few years, missionaries would return to the states for one year and go on tour, hopping from church to church raising funds for themselves and the mission. This time was called "furlough," and my family had our first one in the summer of 1999. Missionaries have always enjoyed a romanticized and almost heroic status among Christians, and we were treated like royalty in the churches we toured. Our visits would occasionally line up with a church's "missions month." Every church had one of these month-long events where each Sunday, different missionaries would speak to the congregation and share their testimonies. For those not fluent in Christianese, a testimony is one's own conversion story followed by what work they are currently doing to advance the kingdom of heaven. I was always fascinated by their stories, specifically their pre-conversion lives. I had been a Christian ever since my parents told me that I was at the age of 4. Some of my earliest memories are of waking up each morning in Wisconsin and running to the window to see if Jesus had come back yet. I was enthralled by the lives that these missionaries had lived before they "met Christ." They told of a life filled with sex, drinking, and uncertainty. Nomadic sojourners searching for truth. Violent ex-marines who had run-ins with the law after getting out of the military. Even my mom and dad's stories seemed like a world apart from mine. However, each narrative would reach a point about halfway through where the momentum would crash. "Then one day I met Jill who invited me to church. At first, I was like, 'no way, man, church ain't for me.' But God must have softened my heart because, after a couple weeks of her asking, I finally gave in and went." Without fail, their story would become colorless and bland from that point until they reached the mission field. Then their energy would pick back up, and the narration would regain some excitement as they described dark rituals and evil ways of the soon-to-be saved godless heathens.

The upright and righteous Christian life was supposed to be the paragon of existence, but no one was capable of describing it in any way that made it sound at all appealing. I repressed these feelings as temptations of the Devil. I certainly wanted the clarity of purpose that came with following Jesus. My flesh was still too sinful; that had to be it. Why else would the very best possible life sound so dull? Despite my self-assurances and the confidence of those around me, I couldn't help but feel somehow cheated. Feeling short-changed by the very thing that was guaranteed to bring joy was a sensation I would revisit later that summer shortly after seeing *The Phantom Menace* for the first time.

Chapter 7

The Russian Counter-Revolution

I grew up in the era of youth group where we all Kissed Dating Goodbye. I remember one time in youth group we came up with the term "Purity Pirates" and I can't tell you how cringey that makes me feel sitting here today. It was designed as this "fun" way to check ourselves before we walked out the door – centered mostly on the oppression of female sexuality due largely to the fact that apparently little Christian boys couldn't look at a girl the way God made her without "stumbling." So that in turn became us – as females – responsibility to shut it down. I remember one year at camp I wore a halter top (whereas I typically had a tendency to be more of a tomboy) and one of my best friends at the time wrote me a long letter about how I was in so many words – acting like a slut. That seems helpful, right? They drilled purity into our heads so hard that I'm pretty sure I developed a complex about relationships. I started to think, "If I even have one emotional feeling about this person, I gotta SHUT IT DOWN OR MARRY THEM!!" because that's completely rational, right? Honestly the thing I feel the most when I look back at youth group as a whole is somewhat robbed of something beautiful. Robbed of being led in how to cultivate a passionate, romantic, frustrating, realistic relationship with God and robbed of blossoming as a beautiful woman. I feel like early youth group suffocated the passion out of women/girls and made us believe we were too much but yet also left us feeling like not enough. A battle I still fight to this very day.
Bobbi, Hawaii

Fundamentalist Evangelicalism suffered a bit of a PR problem after the Civil War. Their insistence on an inerrant and literal Bible drew sidelong glances in the era of Charles Darwin and

Charles Lyell. That would make a great sitcom, *Charles & Charles*. Two scientists get up to all sorts of nutty shenanigans together, like accidentally eating the last tortoise on the way back from the Galapagos or miscalculating the Earth's age by 40 billion years, you know, fun stuff. Anyway, belief in a personal deity who created the cosmos or that a talking snake was responsible for all humanity's woes seemed more the property of a fairy tale than a serious understanding of how the world worked. That being said, American civil religion was still alive and well. The vast majority of people attended church and professed a belief in some form of Christianity.

Fundamentalist Evangelicalism maintained its fringe nature through the majority of the coming century. While other mainstream Protestants were feeding the poor and even advocating for progressive social reforms, fundamentalists preferred a head-in-the-sand approach. The age of the atom appeared poised to eradicate the Christian offshoot entirely. But one little thing sandwiched in the middle of the Great War altered that trajectory entirely.

In 1917, revolutionaries succeeded in ousting the Russian monarchy, and by 1923 the Soviet Union was established. In the space between 1917 and 1923, several experiments with democracy took place in Russia. Workers formed independent groups across the country called Soviets. The Soviets would elect representatives who would then vote in the newly formed Russian Constituent Assembly. However, the assembly was forcefully disbanded after only its second congress by Lenin and his Bolsheviks. The Bolsheviks represented a right-wing counter-revolution to the leftist Soviet revolution. The Bolsheviks controlled most of the armed forces but were outnumbered by leftists in the assembly. Lenin decided democracy was a good thing, but maybe they had a bit too much of a good thing. Apparently his Marxist roots only went so deep. Lenin's authoritarian streak was apparent when he "temporarily" banned any fracture inside the Communist Party. A ban that lasted until 1989. By 1918 almost every other popular political movement was crushed, and the country had been turned into a labor army serving under a single leader. Lenin's death in 1924 and Stalin's subsequent assumption of power put authoritarian governance in the USSR well on its way to absolute.

From the beginning of the October Revolution, the United States backed the anti-communist White Guard, even going as far as having the 339th infantry engage with the Bolsheviks. This antagonism lasted long into the Second World War and was intensified by Stalin's nonaggression pact with Hitler. After the Reich decided to make good on some old WWI grievances, invading the Soviet Union, Stalin made up with the Allies. This alliance was tenuous at best, and when the Allies continuously reneged on their promise to open a second European front, relations degraded even further. The Allies were always uneasy with their Russian comrades, and throughout the war vital information was often withheld. By the time D-Day finally came around, the USSR had already broken the back of the Nazi war machine and lost millions of lives in the process.

Before the war, the outside world watched as a fledgling Soviet Union floundered. The newly introduced agricultural collectivization resulted in massive famines and millions of lost lives. However, their failures were soon eclipsed by incredible success. The Communist Party would take the least developed nation in Europe with a military that bumbled its way through the First World War and turn it into a war machine that would defeat the Nazis and an economic powerhouse. In the course of 40 years, the USSR went from a state of pre-industrialization to putting the first man in space and contending with the US for global hegemony. None of this success was supposed to be possible by American capitalist understanding. Somehow the state hardest hit by the war with over 26 million casualties was outpacing the US in the space race and potentially global influence.

This shallow dive into Soviet history is important for two reasons. One, it provides a basic backdrop for the beginning of US-Soviet relations, without which the resurgence of fundamentalist Evangelicalism would make little sense. Two, Soviet history is really cool. In the early twentieth century, the United States had a strong socialist presence complete with an active political party that was not only accepted by mainstream America but was considered mainstream itself. The Socialist Party of America put over a hundred mayors in office, dozens of state legislators, a couple of congressmen, and plenty of other public officials. They even ran a fairly popular candidate for president. When the party objected to America's involvement in WWI, they suffered a loss in popularity from accusations of cowardice. Interesting side note, the infamous limit to free speech, "you can't shout fire in a crowded theatre," was coined by Supreme Court justice Oliver Wendell Holmes, Jr. when he ruled against the Socialist Party's protest of the WWI draft in Schenck v. United States. The case made it an act of sedition to speak out against the draft.

The Russian Revolution further split the American Socialist Party as many members held vastly different ideological views. Ranging from things like, "the revolution shouldn't happen in Russia – it needs to be Germany," to "Lenin is a bully," to "we need to support the revolution with arms and spread it to America!" In 1917, the US marshals raided party branches across the country, claiming the American Socialist Party to be a seditious organization. However, none of the hardships thus faced would compare to the ones yet to come.

The USSR never claimed to be a communist state. It was governed by the Communist Party, but they called themselves socialists and viewed communism as something yet to be achieved. They also called themselves a people's democracy. In reality, the USSR never truly exited what Lenin called "state capitalism." Lenin viewed state capitalism as a positive stage moving toward socialism but did not believe socialism had yet been achieved. However, while the United States laughed off the democracy part, they latched onto the idea that the USSR was socialist. After Lenin died, Joseph Stalin claimed the USSR had finally achieved true socialism despite the fact that, by nearly every measure, they had regressed further from the socialistic ideals espoused early on. America said the authoritarian and repressive USSR was socialist to defame the concept of socialism, never mind that bit about democracy. The USSR claimed to be both socialist and the purest form of democracy to maintain a facade of operating under the people's mandate. When the only two superpowers in existence agree on a lie, that lie becomes the truth.

The US put their considerable means into fighting the spread of socialism internationally and domestically. On the home front, they conducted raids and countless show trials, locking up suspected communists. They created the very un-American House Committee on Un-American Activities (HCUA), which had wide-ranging powers. Fear of legal action created Hollywood blacklists and led to both state-sponsored and self-inflicted censorship. American playwright Arthur Miller compared it to the Salem witch trials. The difference being that while only 20 people were convicted in that travesty of justice, the "Red scare" resulted in thousands of ruined lives and widespread panic. Another tool in the arsenal of the state was America's civil religion and its fiery fundamentalist undercurrent.

The Soviet Union was officially atheistic, although, from Stalin's reign onwards, they maintained close ties with the Russian Orthodox Church. A church in which Stalin had attended seminary years prior. To help sway popular opinion away from any form of socialism, the US government launched a propaganda campaign effective enough to be the envy of the Glavlit. If communism became synonymous with godless socialism, America would cement its identity in godly capitalism. McCarthy called for jihad in his 1950 Wheeling speech, demanding an "all-out battle between communistic atheism and Christianity." In a fever dream of the Civil War, the government started pumping religious terminology into speeches and religious symbology into the public sphere. Students received a dose of anticommunism each school day after Congress added "One nation under God" to the pledge of allegiance in 1954. Congress also decided to one-up Lincoln by adding "In God We Trust" to every bit of American currency in 1956. "E Pluribus Unum" "Out Of Many One," sounds like pinko bullshit anyways. Courthouses that didn't already sport a ten-commandments etching or religious effigy soon got one.

Eisenhower won his 1952 presidential election in part by championing America's view of itself as a God-fearing city on a hill. He posited America's policy of containment as "a war of light against darkness, freedom against slavery, Godliness against atheism." Eisenhower himself was never very religious, although he claimed to be, as part of his push against communism. Historically, America needed little prompting to split along denominational lines. Protestant vs. Catholic, Baptist vs. Southern Baptist (SBC), and so on. Yet, in this new arena, most denominations and sects could agree that any God was better than no God, thus forming a loosely knit coalition.

Under Ike, the FBI launched the infamous domestic Counterintelligence Program (COINTELPRO). COINTELPRO was tasked with combating all dissenting groups in America, primarily left-leaning dissidents. The powers given to the program were as vast as they were vague. Everyone from MLK to the KKK were in their purview. Though one of these received far more attention than the other. Before COINTELPRO was exposed by a group of courageous burglars who broke into FBI headquarters in 1971, the program was responsible for extrajudicial killings, arming extreme right-wing militias, wiretapping, and a host of other illegal activities. COINTELPRO also did their damnedest to heighten race tensions in a push to turn public opinion away from any form of racial equality and leftist ideology in general. Presidents used the program to spy on rivals and pursue racist agendas. The Church Committee was tasked by Congress in 1975 to investigate abuses by intelligence agencies. What they uncovered made Watergate seem tame in comparison. Ultimately, next to nothing in the way of accountability or justice came from the investigation. The damage had been done. Leftist political movements were destroyed, social justice campaigns had their leaders blackmailed, arrested, or killed. COINTELPRO took a particular dislike to any left-leaning religious black leaders like MLK or the entirety of the Southern Christian Leadership Conference. Black preachers who were fighting for social justice were often dismissed, if not obstructed, by their white counterparts. Any demand for societal change in the era of Marxist revolution was greeted with suspicion.

Ike's spiritual mentor and "America's Pastor" Billy Graham did not mince his words on the topic of communism. In the August 1954 edition of H.L. Menken's influential magazine *The Mercury,* he had the following to say, "It is a battle to the death: either communism must die, or Christianity must die..." But wait, it gets better. He continues with:

Has it ever occurred to you that the Devil is a religious leader and millions are worshipping at his shrine today?... The name of this present-day religion is Communism...The Devil is their god, Marx their prophet, Lenin their saint and Malenkov their high priest...Will we be led by Jehovah God – or duped by Satan? The battle lines are clearly drawn.

Billy Graham spoke to millions over the radio, and in the tradition of Whitefield, Edwards, and Davenport he also took his show on the road. He was so immensely popular that he filled stadiums across the country and around the globe whenever he spoke. Billy Graham's spirited denunciation of communism played no small role in helping America make up its mind about socialism. It wasn't simply the connection between atheism and communism that Billy Graham despised. He spurned any endeavor for an earthly egalitarian society as unattainable and even dangerous. After refusing to take part in the 1963 March on Washington, Graham dismissed the whole endeavor by saying, "Only when Christ comes again will the little white children of Alabama walk hand in hand with little black children."

Paralleling the rise of socialism, Evangelical fundamentalism was slowly metastasizing in America. Needing to hash out the core tenets of their beliefs, Evangelical fundamentalists formed the World Christian Fundamentalist Association (WCFA) in 1919. Turns out that there was no critical theology that separated them from mainstream Protestantism; it was primarily their rejection of modernity that set them apart. They saw the world as having rejected God and viewed pretty much anything new or progressive as evil. In short, Christianity was defining itself by what it stood against, not what it stood for. A stance which excluded anyone who happened to prefer living in the twentieth century. Still, not all Evangelicals were roped into this burgeoning tour de force.

The prominent Evangelical pastor Harry Fosdick preached a sermon entitled *Shall the Fundamentalists Win?* where he labeled the powerful group as both "antimodern" and "anti-intellectual." He feared that all of Christianity was being taken in by reactionary fundamentalism and hoped to put a stop to it. Before you get all dewy-eyed over anti-fundamentalist Evangelicals, remember it was these "Neoevangelicals" who gave us progressive rockstar Billy Graham. Perhaps the most significant aspect of the newly congealed fundamentalist movement was that it marked the first time that Evangelicals became politically active as a group.

A leader in the WCFA and politician, John W. Butler, helped whip up Evangelical support in Tennessee for his 1925 Butler Act. The Butler Act made the teaching of evolution illegal in public schools, directly resulting in the infamous Scopes Monkey Trial. An enthralling bit of history and the subject of several fantastic books. Virtually the entire trial was a publicity stunt. The prosecution and defense were in cahoots to make the whole trial as interesting as possible, and the ACLU sponsored it to make a free speech claim. Scopes never actually taught evolution and was, in fact, only a PE teacher. Seriously, look into this case, it's fascinating. The facts of the suit mattered not at all when it came to pop culture. A fictionalized account of the trial was made into the Academy Award winning film *Inherit the Wind*. The film fixed the Scopes Monkey Trial in the public consciousness as a battle between science and religion. Which is extra weird because the film isn't even about that, it is primarily a critique of McCarthyism. Once again, layer upon layer of misunderstanding and mistranslation ends up a primary mover in culture, not the facts. As a result, fundamentalists suffered another small PR problem. Anti-science was not the stance to be taken in a newly developing high-tech age. Evangelicalism, as a voting block, pulled its head back into its shell, for now.

The concerted effort to weaponize Christianity that stemmed from the Red menace was more successful than anyone could have hoped, and served as a model for other clandestine international campaigns. The CIA, to varying degrees of success, militarized Buddhists across southeast Asia to combat communism, did the same with Catholics in Vietnam, Muslim fundamentalists in Afghanistan, and right-wing Christians all over South America. No group was unsavory enough to warrant second thoughts when communism was the foe. In America, fundamentalism was still regarded as hickish, but as a whole, Christianity became more intertwined in American identity than it had been since the Civil War. Granting a new mob of charismatic, fundamentalist preachers converts in the millions. Technology gave these men modern tools with which to work. The unstoppable success of preachers like Billy Graham inspired hundreds of others to make the jump to radio and then to television.

In 1963, the Supreme Court ruled in Abington School District v Schempp that mandatory devotional Bible readings were unconstitutional in public schools. The ruling did allow for the objective and secular teaching of any and all religions in the classroom. This important and necessary caveat wasn't good enough for Evangelicals. The mother who brought the suit before the Supreme Court won more than just the case, also winning the title of "most hated woman in America." Naturally, Billy Graham had something to say on the subject as well. He complained that the Supreme Court was wrong in their decision and that good Christians were being "severely penalized." Yet another example of inclusivity being viewed as an attack on religious liberties. To date, there have been over 150 drafts of legislation attempting to overturn the court's ruling. Thankfully all have failed thus far. Which remains a thorn in the Evangelical psyche. Several of my childhood friends own and have recently worn shirts that read:

Dear God,
Why do you allow so much violence in our schools?
Signed a concerned student.
Dear concerned student,
I'm not allowed in schools.
God

I grew up believing atrocious anecdotes similar to those t-shirts. I was taught that events like the Columbine shooting resulted from a nation turning away from God. As a Christian, it was my responsibility to interject God back into a decaying country.

A sentiment currently being held by Christian nationalist initiatives like "Project Blitz."

Organized by a Texas group ironically called Wallbuilders, the Congressional Prayer Caucus Foundation, and the National Legal Foundation, Project Blitz's sole purpose is to imbue the classroom with Christian nationalism. Their intent is made disturbingly evident in the 148-page manifesto that supporters hand out to legislators and allies. The document spells out the group's three-prong battle plan to: "protect religious freedoms" by limiting the freedoms of others, "preserve America's Judeo-Christian heritage," by rewriting American history, and promoting prayer, but only Christian prayer. They have successfully pushed legislation in 12 states making it mandatory for public schools to prominently display "In God We Trust" on their walls. Several other states have legislation in the works and will likely follow suit.

The talking points proposed by Project Blitz have ramifications beyond the classroom. A few of their bad ideas include: federal funding for daycares that exclude non-Christian parents' children, declaring a "Christian heritage week," and dozens of other ill-conceived attempts to codify Christian nationalism on both the state and national level. Perhaps someone in Project Blitz should have stopped to at least question their iconography. The word blitz has long been divorced from its Nazi roots, but it's worth remembering that the very first treaty signed by the Nazi Party was with the Vatican to place German public schools firmly under Christian control.

Youth Group, like homework, owes much of its current prominence to the Cold War. Schools pushed homework down students' throats for fear of being out performed by the Soviets, and churches did likewise. Evangelicals saw school campuses as communist hotbeds and set out to counter the Reds' seditious influence on the young. Take a look at a timeline of youth ministries across Evangelical denominations and you'll notice an interesting trend. An explosion of youth ministries and parachurch organizations took place in the 50s, 60s, and 70s.

Some, like Campus Crusade For Christ, currently known as Cru, were quite candid with their objectives. Founded in 1951 by Bill Bright and his wife Vonette, Cru immediately threw themselves into the fight against communism. In a 1953 issue of the *Campus Crusade Communique,* Bill laid out what the crusade was to combat, "At the present rate the world could become communistic almost overnight." He continued to explain how Christian students were on the frontlines against a horde of Marxist professors who were "advocating the violent overthrow of the American government."

Following Bright's example, esteemed Evangelist Billy James Hargis from Texarkana spearheaded a movement in 1952 to stop the influence of communism on American campuses with the similarly named "Christian Crusade" ministry. Side note: American Evangelicals wouldn't say it in front of a camera, but they love the crusades. They name their sports teams, campus ministries, and chess clubs after them. My Christian school sported a literal crusader on a horse as their mascot. Imagine a bunch of German sports teams named Kristallnacht or a British youth ministry called the Colonizers. Anyway, at the height of his popularity, Billy James was broadcast on 500 radio stations and over 250 television stations. Billy preached regularly about the sins of sex-ed, homosexuality, feminism, liberalism, and communism. In 1953, he traveled to West Germany, so he could release 50,000 Bible verses attached to balloons into the Soviet Union. An act of littering that my Youth Group in Wisconsin would later imitate, but into an even more godless terrain than the USSR: Milwaukee. He also seduced several of his student attendees, including a man and woman who were engaged and only admitted their mutual affairs on their wedding night.

Loren Cunningham created Youth With a Mission (YWAM) in 1960. YWAM serves as a tentacle for a super sketchy organization which puts on the National Prayer Breakfast known as "The Family" or the "Fellowship." Yes, the same "The Family" which is featured in dozens of articles, several books, and the 2019 Netflix docuseries by the same name. YWAM and The Family share more than the notorious "C Street house" in Washington DC.

Most people have heard of the National Prayer Breakfast and would be excused for assuming it was some odd tradition our founders cooked up to make prayer a little less tedious or breakfast a little less chatty. Turns out it isn't even a government function at all, rather it's a private gathering which Washington elites choose to attend. It was created in 1953 by the Fellowship under the direction of several influential men, the most prominent of which were Frank Buchman and his apostle Abraham Vereide. To call Frank a Nazi sympathizer is an understatement. In an interview published on August 26, 1936 by the World Telegram, Buchman made his position crystal clear, "I thank Heaven for a man like Adolf Hitler, who built a front line of defense against the anti-Christ of Communism." Oh and the article was entitled, "Hitler Or Any Fascist Leader Controlled By God Could Cure All Ills Of World, Buchman Believes"

The endorsement of Christian fascism is something both The Family and YWAM continued to propagate over the years. In the 80s, they, along with the good ol' Moral Majority gang, played an important role in organizing Christian support for Rios Montt's genocidal regime in Guatemala. Rios Montt abandoned Catholicism and embraced a form of Evangelicalism on brand with Loren Cunningham's own. He sent an emissary to meet with influential religious-right leaders including Cunningham. After their meeting with Rios's man, Cunningham and his pale-skinned detachment of Evangelical warlords, which included Falwell and Pat Robertson, presented Montt's case to the Reagan administration. Since propping up sadistic megalomaniacs was kind of Reagan's kink it didn't take much convincing.

Virginia Garrard-Burnett captured the spirit that allowed for Rios Montt's Christian soldiers to murder some 200,000 of their fellow Guatamalans in her book *Terror in the Land of the Holy Spirit: Guatemala Under General Efrain Ríos Montt*. She describes a Guatemalan pastor who, while visiting his mother church in California, says, "The Army doesn't massacre Indians. It massacres demons, and Indians are demon possessed; they are communists."

In 2003 YWAM posted on their website a blurb written by Jeff Fountain, head of YWAM Europe. He commemorated Europe Day with a love letter to Frank Buchman, a man who would have much preferred a 1000-Year Reich to a European Union, by writing:

An evangelist with global impact, Buchman was acutely aware of the need for reconciliation between the nations of Europe, and indeed the whole world. He knew that if Germany was not embraced by Christian forgiveness and reconciliation, godless forces of anarchy or communism would fill the post-war vacuum.

I do not believe Mr Fountain was intending euphemism, but "acutely aware of the need for reconciliation" should be read euphemistically.

The Family also continued its admiration of mindless loyalty. Douglas Coe, a longtime leader of The Family, now deceased, expressed his desire to recreate the ideological commitment demanded by totalitarian regimes, but for Jesus. He gushes over the total unity created by autocrats from Hitler to Stalin. He holds up China's Red Guard as an example of total abdication of self for the cause, citing its members' willingness to behead their own mothers in the name of the cultural revolution. Saying, "That was a covenant. A pledge. That was what Jesus said."

Chapter 8

Growing Up

Devotional Journal Entries
June 7, 2003
On Thursday we had the 8th grade party at the YMCA and it was fun. We went swimming and stuff. There were too many girls in bikinis though...very much a temptation and annoying. But I guess it's to be expected at an 8th grade swimming party.
July 13, 2003
I rewrote my testimony the other day and it's a lot better. I integrated the Romans road into it, to give people a chance to understand and accept Christ if I told them my testimony.
August 21, 2003
-God please bring my crush to youth group-
Yesterday was the Awana carnival. I ran a booth. My friend asked her to come to youth group Friday night. This could be the answer to my prayer that we would become friends. I'm hoping so I guess. I wouldn't do it but he insisted upon it so he invited her. Haha. She's supposed to call me. We'll have to see what happens. I prayed that God would do whatever's best, so whether or not she comes, I know it's for the best.
Matt, New Mexico

"Lance," my mother called from outside my door. "You cannot miss first period again, or they won't let you graduate!" "I don't have a first period!" I shouted back a little more aggressively than I felt. "Well, the first period of your school day then." "I know, mom!" After a long pause I heard her turn and go back up the stairs. I moved into the basement at the beginning of my senior year hoping to avoid these kinds of confrontations. That was very optimistic of me. No one cared who showed up for school in the last 2 weeks anyways. We had already taken finals, and grades were in.

My mother needn't have bothered waking me up. I had been lying there awake for the better part of an hour staring at the ceiling. It was beginning to dawn on me that there was to be no transfer of clairvoyance upon receiving my diploma. I would be as unsure of my future on the day after graduation as I was lying there in bed.

The previous few years had been a mixed bag for me. We had moved back and forth from Panama several times, and I had transitioned from my Christian boarding school to a private Christian school to being homeschooled, then back to the boarding school, then finally to public high school at the start of my tenth-grade year. I hated high school until halfway through my junior year when my social prospects began to change.

Upon arriving at Lincoln Northeast High School, the only clique immediately accepting of someone as peculiarly abnormal as I definitely was, turned out to be the darkly-dressed and spiky-collared goth kids. They were the first openly non-Christian friends I ever made. Northeast had its own unique strain of goth. Perhaps best described as a 60/40 combination of candy kid culture with post-punk pothead. Raves and ecstasy were weekend staples. However, not for me. I only went to one of these raves, where I refused all proffered drugs while lurking awkwardly in a corner worrying that the music might damage my ears. These guys were anti-everything but didn't really care what you believed in as long as you were relatively nice and never said anything negative about Nine Inch Nails, Tool, or SlipKnot. Unfortunately, they were none too keen on education or giving much of a shit about anything, except for the aforementioned bands.

The goths even stuck with me after I took part in the yearly humiliation of See You at the Pole (SYATP). SYATP is when all the courageous Christian teens gather together before school, hold hands, and pray around the school's flagpole. The event was created in 1990 by SBC youth leaders. To maintain its dubious legality, it has to be student-initiated and led. To remove any hint of non-student leadership, SYATP's website credits its creation to a student-led "brainstorming session" during a youth retreat in Texas.

My school had its flag pole in the middle of the steps leading to the front door. Participation in the event was usually guilt-driven. I had grown up with stories of missionaries achieving martyrdom rather than denying Christ, and Christians in the colosseum being eaten by lions or burned alive for their faith. All I was being asked to do was humiliate myself quite literally in front of the entire school for about 15 minutes. I believed the martyrs had it easy.

I did eventually exit the goth clique. The motivation for doing so rested on a single factor, pretty girls. All the pretty girls who had at one point been goth kids did not remain so once they discovered that they might indeed be a pretty girl themselves. The few pretty girls who stayed in JNCOs and pigtails were in such high demand that I decided to take off the studded belt and black t-shirt to search for greener pastures.

The goth kids were a surprisingly progressive bunch, especially for a small high school in Lincoln, Nebraska. The term "nonbinary" did not really exist yet, but many of my friends would have identified that way if it had. A label that did exist was "bi," and the unattainable goth girl whose attention I had unsuccessfully sought after for 2 years identified as such. My lack of progress in locking down a goth girlfriend eventually inspired my departure from gothdom. A lack of success which might be attributed to a single conversation. I still cringe when remembering my attempt to explain how God loved her as a person but hated her "homosexual lifestyle." The rationale for my exit must sound incredibly shallow, and it was, but the move proved ultimately to be in my best interest.

I found myself casteless in the interim, which in high school is akin to having visual symptoms of syphilis at an orgy. Lunch once again took on the desperate nomadic wandering of my first year in high school when it was not uncommon to eat my sack lunch in a bathroom stall. Social seating arrangements were strictly enforced by disdainful looks and audible grunts. I was a brave kid, but not yet brave enough to sit down where I was unwanted.

On Monday, December 5, in the year of our Lord 2005, I was asked to lunch by Samantha Arlington, who was the single hottest girl at Lincoln Northeast High School. Perhaps the entire Lancaster County school district. I got into a Toyota Camry with two other girls. I did not sit in the backseat, no my friends, I was directed to the passenger seat. I sat in a daze as we drove to Amigos on 48th street. I ordered two cheesy quesadillas without beans and a side of tots. I had made it. Somehow, I was now one of the cool kids.

Turns out I was not one of the cool kids. I was merely accepted by the cool kids. Perhaps only tolerated. I did not frequent the cool-kid parties nor make out with any of the cool-kid girls. As far as I can gather, what must have happened was that the cool kids voted by a thin margin in one of their biweekly meetings to allow me to tag along as a conversation piece. I was more than okay with the arrangement.

The newfound social mobility, while nice, did not change my life. I still spent almost all my free time in my best friend's basement playing video games and watching recorded episodes of *The Simpsons*. Mike and Mark were brothers and the three of us were inseparable in those years. We met at Youth Group and attended every church event, youth retreat, and Bible camp together until the end of high school.

Youth Group remained the epicenter of my social life. I rarely saw anyone from school off campus. I honestly preferred it that way. I didn't know how to handle myself around normal people.

One Friday night, I was invited to a party at Sam's house. I showed up to find it was a slumber party, and I was the only boy in attendance. I was also the only one not wearing pajamas. This was the same fantasy which had played through my mind an embarrassing amount of times. Whatever might have happened was cut short by my severe insecurity. I attempted to blend into the furniture for around an hour before mumbling about being expected at some "college party" then leaving.

Youth Group was where I was free to be myself, as long as "myself" was a God-fearing, energetic proponent of Youth Group. The heliocentric hierarchy of Youth Group placed me on a trajectory for missionary work or to be a youth pastor. I started taking on more and more leadership roles in my church. I even went with Mike to visit NTM Bible school in Waukesha, Wisconsin. I was more than a tad turned off by the strictly enforced no-commingling rules. I was assured it really wasn't that bad, "it's not like Pensacola Bible College, where men and women can't even use the same sidewalk," Brad, my host, had told me.

I was no stranger to rigidity when it came to appropriate relations with girls. My Youth Group was not as bad as some. Hugs were allowed, and even sitting next to a girl on the couch was acceptable. While the undue responsibility of not causing their "brothers to stumble" was still placed on the girls, at least we were told it was our duty not to react if we were to see an uncovered shoulder or upper thigh. I remember once after an outing with the Youth Group to Star City Shores, an incredibly lackluster waterpark which was affectionately nicknamed Star Shitty Sores, my youth pastor told a group of the guys that if we were not aroused by being that close to girls in bikinis it was because we were already too far gone in lustful sin.

Conversations about the scourge of pornography were not limited to our Thursday morning fast food confessionals. On the way back from Star Shitty Sores, our youth pastor told us that one of the worst moments in his life was when he had to confess to his then fiance that he had, on occasion, looked at "internet porn." Hoping to spare us his shameful agony, he implored us "not to go down that road." There was real guilt in his voice. He was old enough to have been without access to the internet for most of his life. The rest of us were presently living in the worldwide web's gilded age. Napster, LimeWire, albinoblacksheep, homestarrunner, KaAza, Morpheus, AIM, Soulseek, rotten.com, ebaumsworld, a few porn sites that utilized more bandwidth than all of South America, and toward the end, Myspace. If he was distraught by the light dusting of pornography that he had consumed, how much more badly should we feel? We internalized his guilt, which only served to bolster our own. There was a decent period that extended from high school onwards where I would literally shake while begging God for forgiveness after watching some very vanilla porn. Having recently spoken to the guys from my Youth Group, I can attest that we all spent our high school years racked with guilt and furiously praying to be forgiven. A fellow Thursday morning disciple grotesquely yet accurately summed up our experience when he recently told me that he "felt like it was our semen sticking Jesus to the cross."

My youth pastor's concern with rectitude was not limited to our uprightness. He had previously told us about a college mentor he had back at Grace University. In his stories it came across that there was a falling out of sorts. On a Wednesday night where the lesson had something to do with being a good example, he told us what had marked the end of their relationship. The only part of the story I can recall is so befuddling as to make all other details irrelevant anyway. Apparently, after some irksome incident, his mentor had exclaimed, "Shit!", and in my youth pastor's own words. "At that moment, I lost all respect for him." I do not want to throw the baby out with the bathwater. My youth pastor was a good guy. He cared for us deeply but was himself only 23 years old, a missionary kid, and from what I could tell, the product of an intensely fundamental upbringing.

I was confident that some Christian leadership role was an unavoidable reality in my future. In an attempt to help us sort out our callings, my youth pastor had us all take a spiritual gifts test which he had found online. The gift of leadership, the gift of healing, the gift of mercy and so on. Somehow I was determined to have the gift of exorcism. This was before Buzzfeed, so the legitimacy of the test is questionable. Important information: My Disney princess is Mulan and I am house Gryffindor.

A popular event for Youth Groups across the Midwest was a massive traveling extravaganza entitled "Dare 2 Share." It has recently undergone an operation similar to that of The Learning Channel's transition to "TLC." Dare 2 Share is now sporting the much more hip name of D2S. One can only assume DTS was not selected because of its proximity to the much more popular acronym DTF. Every year, Dare 2 Share would pop up in Lincoln, NE for 2 days and fill the Lancaster Event Center with thousands of Evangelical teenagers from around the Midwest. It was a massive concert featuring prizes, skits, and motivational speakers. Once lured in by the siren songs of bands like 1000 Foot Krutch, Rebecca St. James, and Third Day, there would be a skit centered upon a modern-day depiction of Christ's crucifixion.

The sketch ends in a climactic shout of "forgive them Father, they know not what they do!" A single drum beat and complete darkness consumes the arena. Center stage, a lone spotlight illuminates a masculine yet unintimidating figure. "That was a pretty cool performance, but you know what's not cool? Sin. It was our sins that put Christ on the cross. It was that little swear word, that white lie, those few clicks on Napster that He died for. But Jesus didn't stay dead, did he?" Resounding "no." "Now, I want everyone to shut their eyes." Cue slowly building instrumental music. "If you feel in your heart the guilt of sin, that awful shame, and you want Jesus to come take that away, I want you to raise your hand. Nobody is looking." We are all looking. "My team and I want to pray with you, if you have your hand raised and you want to accept Jesus into your life, or if you feel you have strayed and want to rededicate your life to *Him*, come on down." An utterly predictable formula but a very effective one. Hundreds of emotionally charged teenagers would shuffle down to the stage for prayer. The day would end with another lively performance before being reminded to show up the next day.

Day two was when things really got interesting. More music, a skit about sharing your faith and being made fun of for it. A recitation of the Great Commission. Then, around 7000 teenagers were tasked with proselytizing to as many people as possible for the next couple of hours before returning to share their stories. Any accounts of "persecution" were awarded with stage time as well as extra points, presumably on Earth as well as in heaven. Before being released upon unsuspecting strangers to nonconsensually share the "good news," the hordes of feverish teens were once again peppered with exaltations of "If you are insulted for the name of Christ, you are blessed" and "Blessed are those who are persecuted for righteousness' sake, for theirs is the kingdom of heaven."

Living in a world where having people not like you meant you were doing something right was not unfamiliar to the majority at Dare 2 Share. So, we went out to win souls and hopefully, if we were lucky, get our asses kicked. I had never been comfortable with the whole tag 'em and bag 'em approach to sharing the gospel, so I found a small coffee shop to hunker down and feel guilty in. Honestly, I had never felt good about any kind of evangelizing. Similar to when I listened to people's testimonies in church, I sensed that what was on offer wasn't the greatest gift imaginable but rather a protracted and tedious chore. I would have never allowed myself to fully conceptualize this thought, but looking back, it best describes my disposition.

No one had their ass kicked. There were a few stories of people stuck in line at the bank or pharmacy getting reasonably upset when young officious evangelists took advantage of a captive audience. All instances of confrontation were easily attributed to the rather understandable annoyance generated by hundreds of entitled teenagers running around "saving" people.

The feeling of being besieged on all sides at all times was paradoxically exhausting and exhilarating. Evangelicals truly believe that there are forces, both of this world and of hell, trying to destroy them on a daily basis. Many of these forces are so insidious as to be undetectable without God's help. I took the directive from the pulpit to be in constant prayer very seriously. I would hold hour-long one-sided conversations with God multiple times in a single day. Usually, it was to beg for forgiveness or to determine the godly choice in a future decision. Both were exercises in futility. If I could regain the time I spent sorting God's will from my own, I would probably live an extra 5 years, possibly another 15 if the prayers for atonement were returned to me. In the tradition of Evangelical analogy, a youth pastor tried to explain our relationship to God in the following way, "Imagine every time we sin as a brick being laid between you and God. Enough sin and the wall is too thick to feel God's presence. But Jesus is like a wrecking ball! When you pray for forgiveness, he sweeps in and tears down that wall of sin!" Thinking back on this analogy I can't help but imagine Jesus as a naked Miley Cyrus swinging in to save my soul.

My Youth Group was fond of outings and events like D2S. Every Youth Group was. The social pressure of being surrounded by like-minded peers was an effective lasso for pulling anyone back who began to stray. No other youth event could compare to the annual escape of summer camp. For much of America's youth, the beloved tradition of summer camp had lost its predominance by the mid-00s. Not so for Evangelicals. Every Youth Group had its preferred summer camp. But we did not call them summer camps; to us, they were Bible camps. Nebraska is littered with enough Christian camps to suit all but the most refined theological palate. Camp Calvin Crest for the no-nonsense Calvinists, Camp Maranatha for the megachurch Evangelicals, Timberlake Ranch Camp for the horsey Christian girls, Camp Luther for the kids who got in too much trouble elsewhere, and my alma mater, Camp Rivercrest, for the less well-to-do Evangelical and occasional Pentecostal. My church's pastor sat on the board of directors for the camp, and almost the entire Youth Group attended each summer. I looked forward to camp every year, and when I was too old to be a camper, I became a camp counselor with three of my best friends and fellow Extreme Remedy attendees, Mike, Mark, and Brandy. What exactly encouraged such recidivism? Imagine the hijinks of *Wet Hot American Summer* meets the brainwashing of *Jesus Camp*.

I was in 7th grade when I first went to Camp Rivercrest, and I returned each year that I was in the country until I graduated high school. My 10th grade year was particularly noteworthy because I had my very first girlfriend attending camp with me. Brandy was an irregular Youth Group attendee before her family moved to Texas 3 weeks before camp started. Her mother was unwilling to pay the $300 tuition or arrange for her transportation back to Nebraska for camp. I conspired to raise the necessary funds by lobbying every old church lady in the congregation. "Ma'am, would you please donate a few dollars to help impoverished children attend camp so that they too can hear about our lord and savior?" It only took me two Sundays to guarantee us a whole week without parental supervision and barely present camp counselors. It was a glorious summer.

An entire division was created by camp administration to capture the likes of Brandy and me. It was called the "Purple Patrol." Their motto: "Boys are blue and girls are pink, let's not make purple!" Later, when Brandy and I returned as counselors, we made sure to head the Purple Patrol ourselves. If you want to get away with breaking the law, the best place to be is on the police force. When we were actually performing official Purple Patrol duties, which was rare, the only perps we ever encountered were fellow camp counselors.

Camp followed a precise schedule meticulously crafted to allow minimal idleness. Some say "the Devil is in the details"; at camp we said "the Devil is in free time." Cabins were cleaned every day before breakfast. Personal devotionals or "devos" immediately followed breakfast which then led to chapel. Chapel was followed by group discussions on whatever godly topic had been addressed earlier in chapel. Then the whole camp would get together for field games before lunch. After lunch, we had a precious 2-hour block of free time before the schedule marched us off into one regimented activity after another. The chipped cog in this finely-tuned machine was the average teenage counselor. As desperate to get away from their responsibilities as we were to get away with making out in the woods, ample time for both was found each day.

Every evening the entire camp would congregate in the chapel for worship and to listen to a message from a man whose only job at camp was to deliver evening sermons. The message at Bible camp followed the same parabolic trajectory year after year.

Monday:
I just want everyone to know how welcome and covered in the love of Jesus everyone here is today!
Tuesday:
Loving Jesus and loving like Jesus are radical ideas! It's not always going to be fun or easy. How many times have you caught yourself falling short?
Wednesday:
You, me, your mom, we are all worthless without God. Jesus died; no, he didn't just die like in a car accident or from a

heart attack. He chose to be tortured to death to save you from that worthlessness. Think about that, Jesus willingly underwent the most gruesome and painful death imaginable so that you, you personally, could experience his love forever in heaven.

Thursday:

Now, with eyes closed and heads down, I want you to raise your hand if, for the first time, you feel compelled today to serve Jesus and want to accept him into your heart. Thank you. Thank you. Heads down, please. If you have already committed your life to Christ but know deep down in your heart that you have strayed and want to rededicate your life to God, please raise your hands. Thank you. At this time, I would like to invite all those who are going through something at home, or have something in your life that you want to lay at the feet of Jesus, maybe it's a divorce or drugs or a sick loved one, just come on forward to the altar where our counselors will pray with you.

Friday:

Did everyone get ice cream?

Having already rededicated my life to Christ each year at camp and several times in between at youth events, I decided to try something new and headed to the altar for prayer. Halfway up the aisle, I panicked upon realizing my parents were not divorced or sick, and I didn't have a drug addiction. I tried to turn around, but the flow of teenagers in need of redemption pressed me forward. I knelt at the altar with my fellow supplicants and awaited the laying on of hands. Thankfully, the number of campers outmatched the number of counselors on hand, giving me time to come up with a sufficiently serious iniquity of which to repent. Glancing to either side, I could see friends, often in tears, huddled with various camp workers. Their hushed prayers and occasional whimpers melding into a single indistinguishable murmur. When my turn came and I felt a firm hand on my shoulder I looked up to see a bald and badly sunburned youth leader looming over me. He gave me an encouraging nod, and I breathed out my shameful confession.

He closed his eyes and began to pray. "Father God!" he shouted loudly enough to gain the attention of not only the Christian God but every single one of the teenagers amassed in the chapel. "We come before you tonight broken and repentant!" I knew everyone was staring at us even before I gained enough courage to look up and confirm it to be the case. My intercessor felt no such disturbance and resumed, "My brother here beseeches you to intervene on his behalf and touch his soul. Please Father God, help Lance break free from..." My mind became a cloud of terror, "No-no-no-no-no-no-no! Please God, no!" The sheer resonance of his prayer must have blocked mine from reaching God's ears because he continued, "...break free from the clasps of lustful masturbation." I felt more eyes tunneling into me and even heard a stifled chuckle. But my attention was quickly ripped away from my surroundings when his prayer continued. "Father God, we know that as men, masturbation without lust is hard and that we should only masturbate as a form of release no more than every 72 hours. But God, we need your help!" The sheer bizarreness rescued me from time and place. I stared at him, absolutely confounded. Yes, masturbation was the sin I had confessed to; it was the most grievous sin I had yet perpetrated against the Almighty, but what on earth was he talking about? The crescendo of his prayer reached an apex and unintelligible babbling burst from his lips. "Baaaah dehm nitty nah ka da da da da ba ba ba ba SHUM! Yes Lord!" Not only had I been gifted with the rare Pentecostal, but one with a very specific and sanctified masturbation routine and the gift of speaking in tongues.

Perhaps on par with summer camp, at least in terms of anticipation, was the ubiquitous endeavor of every well-intended

Youth Group: a mission trip. Most Youth Groups opted for a quick hop across the border to Mexico, or a sun-soaked jaunt in the Dominican Republic. Not so for the ER. After a visiting missionary spoke to the Youth Group during "Missions Week" our minds were set on doing something different, something dangerous. The missionary was on furlough from some war-torn country in the 10/40 window. "Imagine you're at a party and there's one fat kid in the center who everyone keeps giving candy to. All around him are hungry kids who barely get any candy at all. If you're holding a handful of candy, who would you give it to?" We were the candy and the fat kid Mexico. Or maybe Jesus was the candy? See, that's the problem with parables.

Our itinerary in Haiti included painting at a school, helping at an AIDS clinic, working in an orphanage, handing out solar radios that broadcast hygienic information, and converting as many heathens as possible. Mostly important work to be sure. Important enough that maybe it should have been done by someone who wasn't 14 years old. Except for painting that school. We painted the shit out of that school. Similar to NTM in Papua New Guinea, we were converting practicing Catholics. I personally prayed with and converted about 40 Haitians in the 2 weeks we were there. I wonder what confusion there must have been when a white kid shows up with a translator and tells them the story of Jesus, a story they all know by heart, then asks them if they want to accept "Jesus into their hearts." The people in every hut I visited were incredibly kind and accommodating. I'm sure they simply acquiesced out of politeness. No electricity, no running water, no glass or screens in the windows of their homes or even doors, and still they all offered me something to eat or drink. Several times an old woman would order a child to go catch a chicken, so they would have something to feed me. I politely declined, saying I couldn't stay long. Seeing the hovels in which many people lived and the lack of food and water, I felt cruel bringing only words into their homes. The Youth Group raised around $30k for the trip. It's hard not to weigh the potential benefits of simply sending that money to already established local charities against having seven teenagers fumble around at completing tasks. I do not want to come off as overly critical or even cynical. The whole experience did dubious amounts of good and possibly some harm all while further enshrining a white savior mentality. But I can only interpret the smiles and kind words of all the people I encountered as genuine. So many people expressed how much it meant to them to have us come from so far away simply to visit and talk.

Haiti had been experiencing terror raids by right-wing militias throughout rural regions at the time. Shortly after we left the country, there was a coup d'état that ousted President Jean-Bertrand Aristide. Depending on the source, the US either rescued or kidnapped the president then dropped him off in the Central African Republic. The signs of political upheaval were prevalent while we were in Haiti. Streets were perpetually being cleared of barricades and burning tires, gunshots could be heard in the distance. Our minds were elsewhere.

In an act of religious voyeurism, our youth pastor took us to a gathering of Haitian Mambos and Hougans at Bois-Caiman. It was quite the experience. We saw a pit full of gore where some sacrifice had recently been made. A man stood in the center furiously masturbating while covered in oily dark blood. Naturally, we all bought a couple of souvenirs. Later that night, convinced our little trinkets were possessed by Satan we smashed them against a rock. I helped in the destruction but removed my own keepsakes from the carnage. I still have my little green box with "Haiti" engraved on the top.

Evangelicalism suffers greatly from the "white savior complex." We've even bleached *the* savior to match our own skin tone. Growing up in the church, it was my experience that white people, usually men, went to where brown and black people lived to help them become more like us. Not only to save their souls, but to essentially save them from themselves. So much was this my impression that when I first met a black missionary, I assumed one of the white missionaries had brought him back from the mission field. It did not help that one of the few magazines I grew up with was put out by New Tribes Mission and was literally called *Brown Gold*. The magazine retained its problematic name until 2017. Our white savior was grandiose enough to block the sun from shining on any other heroes with a bit more melanin. For example, we were taught Haiti only gained its independence from white men by calling on Satan to fight for them. Toussaint Louverture's brilliant tactics and statecraft had nothing to do with leading the most successful slave revolt since Sparticus. White cultural superiority didn't have to be taught; it was simply understood as true.

Other cultures were treated as quixotic peculiarities at best or tools of the Devil at worst. The private Christian school I attended for 6th grade in Lincoln was entirely without a single person from Mexico, or even a native Spanish speaker, yet would arrange a "Mexican Market" once every school year. Mexican Market was a massive garage sale where kids would gather up any unwanted toys, video games, sports equipment, etc., and sell them from mats in the gymnasium. Our teachers informed us that authentic Mexican markets only sold cheap goods, so a price cap of $10 was set for any single item. We were encouraged to bargain for the lowest price like "real Mexicans." I manned the nacho booth as well as my adjacent mat. I made about $120 that day—a lot for a 6th grader. None of the earnings went to any Mexican charity or even a mission trip; we pocketed every penny. Of course, a culturally insensitive event of this magnitude would not have been complete without students, teachers, and staff wearing sombreros, ponchos, and large false mustaches.

Even with spending the majority of time between my Evangelical family and my Evangelical church, there was a rising cognitive dissonance in my mind. One which had been incubating without my knowledge or consent. If even for a second, I had realized that my fundamentalist worldview was in jeopardy, I would have immediately repented, bought a new daily devotional, and watched several hours of Kent Hovind.

In my church, embracing the theory of evolution was tantamount to blasphemy against the Holy Spirit. Accepting that the planet was in the midst of a man-made ecological disaster was not quite as bad but still outed you as either a liberal or a sucker. I saw myself as one of the few crusaders of truth in my high school – someone who was willing to stand up against the twin behemoths of political correctness and liberal public education.

I picked my battles poorly. Needless to say, both evolution and global warming enjoy an almost indisputable foundation in reality. The educators who cared enough to debate me on these subjects had no problem citing actual evidence. Evidence was something that was a skosh sparse in my corner. Instead, I relied on bewildering opponents, whose intellects were generally far keener than my own, with pure fabrication and sophistry. For example, did you know that on an international level, more money was raised in 2005 to fund climate change studies than OPEC made in that same year? Of course you didn't know that, neither did I, nor anyone else. But it sounded good when I made it up, and more importantly, it fitted into my worldview perfectly. I never questioned why on earth I connected an issue like global warming with my faith at all, or why I considered lying less of a sin than believing in climate change. The important thing was that evolution, climate change, affirmative action, the gay agenda, free healthcare, or whatever else happened to be up for discussion were all hooks the "world" used to snare young Christians. Not this young Christian. I knew God was under attack in America, and I was not falling for it.

There was a certain excitement to the constant imaginary barrage of demonic arrows. Like a spy in enemy territory. The problem was that we lived in arguably the most religiously tolerant nation on the planet. A nation where Christianity held considerable privilege. When I was in Youth Group during the late aughts, self-professed Christians filled almost every level of government from the local level all the way to the presidency. Attorney General and songwriter John Ashcroft had dropped this bomb while accepting a fake degree from Bob Jones University on May 8, 1999:

> Unique among nations, America recognized the source of our character as being godly and eternal, not being civic and temporal, and because we have understood that our source is eternal, America has been different. We have no king but Jesus.

If only the government would stop trying to destroy our religious liberties! At the time Ashcroft was giving his speech, Bob Jones still operated under a gross apartheid. Blacks were admitted but were not allowed to date whites. Not exactly off-brand for the Religious Right. Ostensibly, the constitution guarantees freedom from a state sanctioned religion, when in fact the exact opposite had been happening for almost 30 years. But if we were true Christians, someone had to hate us. Matthew 10:22 made it pretty clear: "You will be hated by everyone because of me, but the one who stands firm to the end will be saved." Bland political disagreements were enough to cry "persecution!" Alternatives to the traditional family made legal? That also treads on my religious liberties. Creationism not being taught with equal validity as evolution? Clearly persecution.

A particularly cringeworthy instance of my being a bulwark for Christ took place on national coming out day. I was sitting in class when over the intercom came an announcement from the student council. I cannot recall the exact phrasing, but it was a well-intended although incredibly ill-conceived call for all those "in the closet" to come out and declare their true selves mid-English class. In a show of pure assholery, I stood up and declared myself as straight then asked "Where's the national I'm straight day?!" It elicited a few giggles from the class and ensured no one else would have any other declarations that day. I'd like to excuse my antics as simple ignorance but unfortunately I cannot. I truly believed that I was making some grand gesture by standing up to the pervasive and culturally perverting "gay agenda." My father still tells this story to dinner guests with more than a little pride in his voice. I feel no such pride. I shared my English class with a girl I'll call Ann. I had known her since middle school. What I did not know was that she was in the middle of coming to terms with who she really was. A couple of years after high school, Ann transitioned into who he had always wanted to be. I've talked to him a few times in the last year or two and am glad to have had the opportunity to apologize for being an ass.

The "gay agenda" was a nebulous and nefarious plot being carried out by secular humanists, liberals, feminists, and the gays. The agenda itself was vague enough to incorporate a wide swath of threats. Primarily, it was a scheme to destroy men.

World renowned Evangelical author and anthropomorphous bag of mayonnaise Dr James Dobson wrote a child-rearing novella entitled *Bringing up Boys*. In this work of art, he states that "masculinity is an achievement" and that men should not be "feminized, emasculated, and wimpified." He believes the gay agenda sets out to do exactly that. Apparently, he has never done much reading on The Sacred Band of Thebes or been to Provincetown during Bear Week. Mr Dobson was the creator of Focus on The Family and is one of the most influential Evangelicals today. In 2000 Focus on the Family contributor and founder of the far-right Evangelical rag *Mission America* Linda Harvey put out a handy 12-point checklist for parents trying to determine if their school was secretly executing the dreaded gay agenda. I went in search of this list because I recalled coming across it in my early teens and even then thinking it was paranoid. On the surface, the so called "Dirty Dozen Checklist" comes off as outlandishly humorous, but be warned, it is also disturbing. For the sake of brevity, I have only included the 12 items themselves and not their rationale for why each is particularly dangerous. According to Linda, your child was at a terrible risk if their school had:

1. A "safe schools" non-harassment program.
2. A homosexual student club.
3. Non-discrimination policy based on "sexual orientation."
4. Programs to stop "homophobia," "hate", or "bias."
5. Pro-homosexual literature added to curricula and libraries; pro-family material bypassed or discarded.
6. AIDS and "safe sex" education programs.
7. Teachers/staff who are openly homosexual. Not positive role models for students. Close student-teacher relationships are high-risk.
8. Involvement in your school of radical pro-homosexual groups like GLSEN, PFLAG, & Lambda Legal Defense Fund. These groups are well-funded and looking for fights. Any objectors will be subject to public disgrace.
9. Celebrating "gay pride" month or "coming out" day There is nothing to celebrate about encouraging kids to adopt dangerous sexual practices.
10. Exhibits/films on families headed by homosexuals. Tries to put a conventional face on problem behavior.
11. Students & parents with concerns being silenced. Intimidation goes hand-in-hand with the expressed goal of "ending homophobia."
12. Teacher in-service meetings promoting diversity and complaining about "homophobia." Often required now by school systems, these programs foster attitudes of hostility toward tradition-minded parents, who are

portrayed as trouble-makers.
——————————————How Does Your School Score?

Sadly, I was forced to remove the key by which to score your results. Again, for brevity's sake. Had I left the list as is, it would fill three solid pages. Surprisingly, *Mission America* still has this list up on their website; I would suggest taking a look. Strict gender roles became a core tenet in Evangelicalism, and any deviation from their interpretation of biblical norms was a clear attack on the family, the country, and God. Linda Harvey's list provides a quintessential example of how Evangelicals viewed not only the "gay agenda" but the world in general. No one was out there trying to force gay sex on the church, but any effort of inclusion was quite clearly viewed as an attack on our religious liberties. Happy holidays, not Merry Christmas? Clearly an attack on Christianity. An emphasis on Black history? Also an attack on Christianity via social engineering! If there was any truth to the "gay agenda," it was simply to have society acknowledge their humanity, to tell all those confused kids out there to stop feeling like they had to apologize for existing. Sadly, Evangelicals' mutation into Christian nationalists had already entered into its last phase, and they were far too caught up in the metamorphosis to acknowledge anyone else's humanity, let alone rights.

Social engineering was a tagline that carried even more weight than the gay agenda. I grew up with stories of how lucky my great-great grandparents had been to emigrate from Russia before the Bolshevik social engineering programs destroyed the country. While being homeschooled, my mother took me to the Germans from Russia museum in Lincoln, where we found records of our ancestors arriving at Ellis Island. We also went to the Telephone Museum and the Rollerskating Museum. The last two were much more fun. In my parents' minds and in the minds of many Evangelicals, social engineering and social justice reforms were the hallmarks of atheistic dictators like Lenin, Stalin, or Mao. The teaching of evolution was akin to Soviet Lysenkoism. Government-mandated desegregation, or any social program aimed at equality, had the backdrop of Mao's Cultural Revolution to contend with. It is in this space where a Venn diagram of far-right political groups and Evangelicals overlapped. Both parties harbored a strong sense of resentment fueled by a belief that they were being marginalized and disenfranchised by a powerful liberal elite. Never mind the stranglehold Evangelicals had on the body politic or how far to the right policy had drifted over the last 50 years.

Religious fundamentalists and right-wing politicians, while winning the political game, were slowly losing the cultural one. Movies, music, and social norms no longer lined up with the strict hierarchy they both clung to. Neither group wanted to see their influence and privilege diminish whatsoever – an impossible goal given their historical dominance in a society now attempting equilibrium. The far right and Evangelicals had slowly been merging for years. In the late aughts the overlap between the far right and Evangelicals widened into a group much more powerful than either were alone. Christian nationalists were soon to make their presence felt.

I was coming of age in the midst of the far right and Evangelicalism coalescing into Christian nationalism. Almost everything in my life was pulling me along a path of extremism. As already demonstrated, I was already a dogmatic asshole in high school. Fortunately, it was becoming nearly impossible to keep my mind entirely shut. When all one has to offer in debates are semi-logical doubts and "creative facts," as a too-kind environmental science teacher once called them, one is forced to question one's beliefs. The school day, which had begun with my mother banging on my bedroom door, concluded with one of my most tightly held beliefs being dented.

There is a magical pocket of time that only exists for a

few weeks before summer break. Most teachers were already completely checked-out. Half my classes consisted of movies, popcorn, and coke. I was running a few minutes late to my first period, then every other period before lunch. As fun as classes were in those last days, passing periods were still better. There is always that one teacher in every school whose contagious passion for learning is impossible to ignore. Mr Crawford, not his real name, wasn't one of those teachers, and I doubt he had ever even conversed with one. He once assigned "doing the newspaper's crossword" every day for a whole week. I only mention Mr Crawford because his class provided the dark backdrop for the shining star that was my AP Lit. class. Ms Sara Skeen was a student favorite despite her tendency to educate until the very last day of school. She was young and shared a wardrobe with *The Magic Schoolbus*'s Ms Frizzle. Sadly, she would die of a rare cancer a few short years after I graduated. Ms Skeen was kinder to me than I deserved, and I always made sure to be on time for her class, which often required several minutes of reckless driving and even more reckless parking to accomplish since I had her directly after lunch.

"What about the kangaroos?"

"What about the kangaroos?" I retorted.

"How did they get to Australia?" Drew said with more of a declarative tone than an inquisitive one.

The question obviously held more meaning than I could quickly sort out. I had debated the topic of evolution dozens of times before, and this was the first time kangaroos had ever made an appearance. Ms Skeen was fond of debates and coached the debate team. With her curriculum exhausted, Ms Skeen would have the class pick topics, and she would moderate debates. We used different structures for debates, this particular one was far from formal. Skeen called it "popcorn debates." She would write the subject on the board, then whoever wanted to speak would raise their hand, and they were allotted a maximum of

2 minutes to make a statement or respond to one. Ms Skeen sat on a stool at the front of the room with her legs crossed. The cork sole of her Birkenstock sandal periodically slapped against her heel as she clenched and unclenched her toes. She wore a long, sleeveless denim dress with quilt patch pockets and a red turtleneck underneath. Her thin, dark hair framed a stern yet caring face. Behind her on the whiteboard was written, "Should evolution be the only theory taught in public schools?" Uncharacteristically, Ms Skeen had allowed for the debate to digress into creative design VS evolution.

"What do you mean, how did they get to Australia?" I asked, trying to avoid answering a question I didn't understand.

Drew was a frail kid who always wore the same t-shirt that cleverly stated that "there are 10 types of people in the world, those who understand binary and those who don't" He sported a bowl cut despite the trend's popularity having died out years prior when J.T.T. had cut his hair on "Home Improvement."

"I mean, if there were two of each animal on the Arc, and that Arc landed on the top of some mountain in the Middle East, then how did those kangaroos get to Australia?" Drew asked again with a smug "gotcha" look on his face. This was something that I never had once thought about. I had read about theorized land bridges, so I jumped at such an easy explanation.

"Land bridges! Several thousand years ago, there was a land bridge to the mainland." I had exactly zero evidence for what I just said, but it was stated with such authority that I was confident not only would my explanation be accepted, but I would save the soul of the heathen by shattering his devil-wrought worldview.

"Even if there was one, which there wasn't, what happened to the skeletons of all the dead kangaroos that once lived in Asia, Africa, or Europe? Or did the kangaroos pick up all the dead bodies and take them with them to Australia?" he asked, not phased at all by my previous gusto.

"Uhh..." My thoughts raced as the new, inescapable reality settled in my mind. "What the fuck happened to the kangaroos?!" kept bouncing around my skull. I swore a lot in my head but rarely in public. These "brain swears" plagued me to such a degree that I once offered them up as a prayer request during a Youth Group meeting. More immediate than angering God with vile thought bubbles was the gosh darned kangaroo dilemma. Not only the kangaroos, though; this would be true of any geographically isolated species. I had to be missing something simple, but nothing came to mind. Without a creative explanation, or an intellectually honest thing to say, I resorted to a cliche I once heard creationist Kent Hovind use. "The absence of evidence is not the evidence of absence." That pushed the conch back to Drew and sounded smart enough to keep me afloat in the eyes of my classmates, who were mostly Evangelicals themselves. It was now his turn to be flustered. He stammered for a moment before Ms Skeen saved us both by declaring it time for a new topic.

The rest of the school day was spent inside a crashing wave. My ears hummed with it. All the blood had rushed to my head as I tried to sort out what was going on. It was as if Drew had unwittingly tipped the largest in a succession of diminishing dominoes. Was truth something that had to be proven with evidence? Did evidence have to be material? Was it counted unto me as righteousness for believing without evidence? Could faith really be boiled down to believing something with insufficient data? If the Bible mentioned God calling all the animals two by two onto the ark, why wouldn't it mention a miracle of spontaneous dispersion? These were brand new questions to me, and I found them profoundly dismaying. By the end of the school day, I had resolved to go on thinking the things that I had always thought, and that faith required me to accept God's word regardless of contrary evidence. However, the problem with a severe case of cognitive dissonance is that you cannot simply decide for it to go away.

Chapter 9

Ronald Reagan

I stopped being an Evangelical years before I stopped being a Christian. I stopped being an Evangelical when I got pregnant. For all their pro-life talk they sure didn't show much support when I chose to keep my baby. I was 16 when my Christian school and my church youth group expelled me. You would think they'd have at least kept me around as a cautionary tale. My school kicked me out for violating a behavioral contract I signed when I was 15 and my youth group expelled me more gently by asking me to "take some time away." It was hard, I kept thinking that if I had chosen to abort, possibly the worst sin an Evangelical girl could make, no one would have known and I wouldn't have to change schools, churches, or friends. Christians drilled into me that pro-life was the only stance to take then punished me for taking it.
Tina, Kansas

Paul Weyrich, the pro-life Catholic conservative from about 50 pages ago, was looking to conjoin Christians with Goldwater conservatives to create a new and powerful voting bloc. He knew there were millions of politically uninvolved Christians all over the country. If he could somehow convince them to get involved, he was sure their conservative religious views would tie them together and provide the very thing needed to put a stop to America's moral decay. Evangelicals only had eyes for heaven. Or so it appeared because there was nothing that Mr Weyrich could use to cajole them into action. That all changed when he came into contact with Robert Billings. Robert Billings was a former missionary and, surprise, surprise, itinerant preacher. He was a big proponent of private Christian schools, or more accurately, white-flight schools. The Supreme Court's ruling in Brown V Board of Education attempted to desegregate the public school system. An uninterded result was a massive boom in private all-white Christian schools. To get an idea of how rapidly white students fled the public school system, take the example of Holmes County, Mississippi. After only 2 years of desegregation in Holmes County, the number of white students in the public schools went from around 700 to 0.

After several court cases established that any organization which engaged in racial segregation was not applicable for tax-exempt status, Mr Billings lost his shit. He created the National Christian Action Coalition (NCAC) and hopped back on the road to preach about the evils of secularism and presumably tax codes. Along the way, he helped to create 400 new lily-white Christian schools. Mr Billings was able to garner massive Evangelical support. Brown V Board of Education, not Roe v Wade, is what brought the Evangelicals out of their 50-year hiatus. Taxes and racism. Of course, it was not presented as such. Mr Billings, and his Evangelical supporters, perceived the government as being guilty of overreach and restricting their religious liberties. A threat to their privileged tax-exempt status could not go unchallenged. The law was upheld, but a new refrain in Evangelicalism was taken up. Any advancement in the rights of others which came with a loss in Evangelical privilege was clearly an attack on religious liberties. Racism may not have been the external motivator, but it is not a coincidence that almost every major Bible school from Moody to Bob Jones was still segregated long past the Supreme Court's denunciation of "separate but equal." There are still hundreds of Christian white-flight schools peppering the country (maybe I should say salting the country) and most churches remain almost entirely segregated to this day.

In 1978, Paul Weyrich pushed his pro-life pet project in several key areas during the midterm elections. He orchestrated the showering of churches with pro-life leaflets days before the election. In all four districts across Minnesota and Iowa where Mr Weyrich was active, pro-life Republicans replaced their Democratic predecessors in the November midterms. Mr Weyrich brought his experimental success to that fateful meeting in 1979 between himself, Robert Billings, and professional racist Jerry Falwell. The Moral Majority was born, and Billings became the executive director.

Almost 4 years before the formation of the Moral Majority, the very Evangelical Jimmy Carter had been elected president. He was not only the first presidential candidate to be so upfront with his personal faith but to also base an entire campaign on it. Evangelicalism had a vocal proponent occupying the most powerful office in the world. However, his policies were still too progressive for the newly crystallizing "New Right." They attacked Carter with the government overreach argument even though it was Nixon who had really gone after private schools for not desegregating. The Moral Majority decided to nail him on his permissive approach to abortion. Like a much less charismatic Robespierre, Carter was destroyed by the very movement he helped create.

At the formation of the Moral Majority, abortion had been legal in all 50 states for over 6 years. The Evangelical community had mixed opinions, but on the whole were not overly upset about its newfound legality. Falwell himself did not preach against it until 1978. The 1971 Southern Baptist Convention put out a resolution on abortion where they implored their congregants to "work for legislation that will allow the possibility of abortion under such conditions as rape, incest, clear evidence of severe fetal deformity, and carefully ascertained evidence of the likelihood of damage to the emotional, mental, and physical health of the mother." Rather progressive stuff for an organization whose very genesis sprung out of a pro-slavery schism with other Baptists in 1845.

So what happened? Well, it's a bit of a ride. Remember those

Neoevangelicals who couldn't stomach the anti-intellectualism of the fundamentalists? The guys who gave us Billy Graham? Turns out Hermann Hesse was correct when he said, "If you hate a person, you hate something in him that is part of yourself. What isn't part of ourselves doesn't disturb us." Because it was the Neoevangelicals, or who the Neoevangelicals had morphed into, that showed up in a big way. While Weyrich was out garnering political support, Evangelical heavy hitter Francis Schaeffer was touring the nation on Jerry Falwell's private jet speaking about several of his different films and books, including most famously *How Should We Then Live?*, *A Christian Manifesto.* and *Whatever Happened to the Human Race?* He attacked every precept of modern life from Darwin to the Renaissance. When it came to influence on the Evangelical world, Schaeffer would eventually take second place only to Billy Graham. Schaeffer was the father of the culture wars. He warned that everything from women's rights, to evolution, to abortion, to removing prayer from schools to gay rights, to euthanasia were the fruits of a shadowy agenda being executed by "secular humanists" with the end goal of destroying America's Judeo-Christian heritage or even Christianity itself. You can hear the taint of conspiratorial thinking in his essay Foundations for Faith and Freedom:

Today the separation of church and state in America is used to silence the church. When Christians speak out on issues, the hue and cry from the humanist state and media is that Christians, and all religions, are prohibited from speaking since there is a separation of church and state...It is used today as a false political dictum in order to restrict the influence of Christian ideas.

Though Schaeffer claimed to detest theocracies, he consistently advocated for one. As a Presuppositionalist, it would be near impossible for him not to. Presuppositionalism is the incredibly humble belief that Christianity provides the only source for rational thought. Jerry Falwell, Weyrich, Billings, and the other Evangelical hitmen at the Moral Majority absolutely loved the idea of combining the causes for every conceivable sin into one easy-to-swallow pill. A pill that could be sold as both Kosher or transubstantial.

Abortion had always been considered to be a Catholic issue, but with Schaeffer's framing they could now form a coalition between Catholics, Jews, and Evangelicals. Abortion wouldn't be an issue if women weren't so damn promiscuous, and they wouldn't be so promiscuous if it wasn't for those damn women libbers, and the women libbers wouldn't exist if we would have just stuck to our not-at-all-mythical Judeo-Christian heritage! Schaeffer's work undoubtedly helped lay the moral foundations for Christian nationalism. However, there were some lines Schaeffer was hesitant to cross. He was insistent that moving too far in a political direction would only serve to cheapen "real" Christianity. In *A Christian Manifesto,* he wrote, "We should not wrap Christianity in our national flag."

A man with no such qualms was Rousas Rushdoony. Rushdoony and Schaeffer shared a belief that America's rejection of Christ underlaid every other problem, but they differed on how to fix it. Rushdoony advocated a complete takeover of the American government by Christians. He believed that the Great Commission was a command to spread Christian dominion over the entire world. This belief is known as "Dominionism." Dominionists assert that Christians must gain absolute authority over the entire planet before Jesus will return.

Rushdoony himself was the father of Christian Reconstructionism, which advocates a global theonomy. Theonomy is a fun word that essentially means a libertarian economic system of government run by God himself. Rushdoony promoted a return to a system of laws similar to the Old Testament. Death penalty for pretty much every offense. He believed it to be the Christian duty to take control of every possible component of daily living. This may all sound absolutely wackadoodle, and it is, but here's the problem. Rushdoony had a brilliant mind. Brilliant in the same vein as Goering, Shirō Ishii, or Ted Kaczynski. Fortunately for us, Rushdoony never occupied a seat of power from which to bring about a return to the crusades. He did, however, greatly influence the thinking of those who do. Many, if not all, Evangelical officials in the Trump administration from Pompeo to Pence have expressed dangerous beliefs rooted in Dominion theology. Find any expressing Evangelical politician today, dig into their past, and you are all but guaranteed to discover a Dominionist background.

Rushdoony's theology influenced my own life in ways I never fully appreciated until I began researching for this book. In part, I have Rushdoony to thank for that great coloring book as a child. In a lecture entitled "Human Nature in its First Estate," he espoused the following concept which is now foundational to almost every Evangelical:

> If creationism is at all weakened, the doctrine of salvation is weakened. Creation and salvation are different sides of the same coin. God has created man, God alone can redeem him. If we tamper with the doctrine of creation we have proportionally weakened the doctrine of salvation.

While Robert Billings was concerned about integration, it was Rushdoony who pushed the evils of public education as "anti-Christian to the core." I was given an almost verbatim explanation when I asked why I was being homeschooled in 7th grade. Rushdoony's name remains a lesser known one, but it's his ideas that have percolated for decades and infected Evangelicalism at its heart. Mr Schaeffer may be the father of the culture wars, but Rushdoony is the father of modern Christian nationalism.

Tapping into American religious anxiety, the new Religious Right was the result of a well-orchestrated agenda. It was not the result of a top-down push nor a grassroots campaign. As with any major social movement, neither the leadership nor the rank and file could exist long without the other. Nevertheless, the strategic alliances made by the leadership were paramount to the New Right's success. A confederacy of politically conservative religious organizations like the "Christian Voice," the "National Christian Action Coalition," the "Religious Roundtable" and of course the "Moral Majority," all funded by large corporate donors, helped get the word out to every church congregant that Satan was out there, and his name was liberalism.

From the end of WWII all the way to 1980, it was almost taken for granted that the political elite, both Democrat and Republican, were essentially liberal. This was universally true in terms of the Keynesian interpretation of the word, and true to varying degrees socially. That all changed when the newly formed Religious Right flexed their collective muscle and put Ronald Reagan in the White House.

In the late 70s, many American cities were experiencing record crime rates. The nation's economy was in shambles. The Soviet Union's power seemed unstoppable. The war in Vietnam ended with worse terms than were on offer in 1968. The president had left office in disgrace. All in all, things were not looking great. Meanwhile, the propaganda push which started in the late 40s and early 50s had led to both a new acceptance of Evangelicals as well as right-wing politics. Evangelicals had the incredibly popular televangelists like Oral Roberts, Jimmy Swaggart, Tammy Faye Bakker, Billy Graham, and Rex Hubbard, all preaching society's sins. The Right was not without their false prophets, William Rusher, Robert Whitaker, and William F. Buckley, to name a few. With incredibly influential men from both groups all pointing their fingers at the same perpetrator of American woes, it was not difficult for figures like Paul Weyrich to rope them together and elect Ronald Reagan.

Reagan's administration gave positions of power to men like Robert Whitaker and angry white guy Robert Billings. Mr Whitaker was a senior staffer and would later become an Alt-Right darling for his creation of the "White Genocide" mantra. You know the one which claims, "anti-racist is a code word for anti-white." While Mr Buckley gets most of the acclaim for the rise of the right, it was his publisher William Rusher whose ideas ultimately had more influence in today's fearful, right-wing populism. His 1988 book *The Coming Battle for the Media: Curbing the power of the media elite* reads like last night's Tucker Carlson episode, except more logically constructed. We are already familiar with Robert Billings. Reagan made Mr Billings his religious advisor during the campaign, then put him in the Department of Education of all places.

The Religious Right under Reagan's tenure was empowered like never before. It was during this time that the Religious Right began to reflect more of an Evangelical Right. The battle cry of abortion had finally been fully embraced by Evangelicals, and the loosely knit coalition with Catholic fundamentalists was not as important as it had been. Catholics were still in the fold, but the Evangelicals were in control. Reagan pandered directly to Evangelicals and this pandering resulted in a swelling of their influence. In 1985, Billy Graham made an appearance on Pat Robertson's ridiculously popular TV show *The 700 Club*, where he pretended Evangelicals were not already pulling the strings:

The time has come when evangelicals are going to have to think about getting organized corporately...I'm for evangelicals running for public office, winning, and getting control of the Congress, getting control of the bureaucracy, getting control of the executive branch of government.

However, the number of people willing to admit to being an Evangelical dropped significantly after several high-profile televangelists were caught up in sex scandals and money laundering in the late 80s. "Evangelical" was already a blanket term for a wide variety of theologies and denominations. Pentecostals, Anglicans, Methodists, Baptists, Anabaptist, Prybeterians, etc etc all found a home there. The disgrace lay with the Evangelical brand not the ideology. People simply went back to identifying with their denomination without having to change any of their Evangelical beliefs. Subsequently, the ignominy did not last long and within a few short years the stain was gone.

Evangelicals were about to find themselves with even stranger bedfellows than they had found in the Catholics. After fighting so tirelessly to put Reagan in the White House, Evangelicals carried on fighting for Reagan's policies. This meant snuggling up to a neoliberal directive as influenced by economist Friedrich Hayek and his apostle Milton Friedman. Jesus may have chased out the money lenders but Evangelicals now invited them in.

Neoliberalism, like Evangelicalism, is a word with a tricky definition. Professor Noam Chomsky summed it up succinctly in his interview with Christopher Lydon for *The Nation* in 2017 by saying, "its [neoliberalism's] crucial principle is undermining mechanisms of social solidarity and mutual support and popular engagement in determining policy." The "mechanisms" he's mentioning range from cultural to economic. Culturally, e.g. defining freedom as the ability to choose which tyrannical employer to work for. Economically, e.g. legislating supply-side or "trickle-down" economics.

The Republicans were primarily a party of the super-rich, and they faced the dilemma of having a new Evangelical base that was not. Friedman, a student of Hayek, sold trickle-down economics to Reagan who bought in so wholeheartedly it soon became known as "Reaganomics." The Carter administration had adopted tenets of neoliberalism, but 40 years of Keynesian economic policy was turned on its head almost overnight with the election of Ronald Reagan. Paul Weyrich's Heritage Foundation helped propagate this new gospel with as much gusto as it hawked Evangelical grievance. Other neoliberal organizations, backed by wealthy capitalists, popped up like canker sores. The Cato Institute, The Institute for Economic Affairs, The Center for Policy Studies, The Adam Smith Institute all existed for one purpose: to inject neoliberalism into every possible entity from universities to high schools to government committees. Privatization is the neoliberal God, and deregulation his only begotten son. Beyond the pearly gates lay monopoly as a just reward for a job well done.

With its emphasis on moving power away from elected officials and toward unaccountable, private tyrannies, neoliberal policy worked wonders for Reagan's wealthy donors and powerful friends. Not so much for the millions of peasants on whose votes he depended. To ensure the Evangelical vote, Republicans switched their emphasis from policy to values. Policy was tricky and could be shown as harmful to the base. Values, that's the ticket. It kept the base from questioning or even recognizing that their real wages were continuously reduced or that they had the highest workload with the fewest benefits of any Western nation. Sweet nothings were whispered into the voter's ear, things like "we're the party of family values, a law-and-order candidate, a defender of American values." Each vague enough to be loaded with whatever meaning the listener decided upon. Republicans' accentuation of values meshed perfectly with the Evangelical presuppositions. No longer beholden to any demonstrable criterion, Republicans were free to run roughshod over the public interest. Not immune to self-enrichment, neoliberalism became the new consensus for the Democrats and Republicans alike.

The American businessman has always enjoyed a special place in Evangelical Americana. Even so, sanctification of the corporation came surprisingly easy to most Evangelicals. Perhaps it was how both the corporate and church structures lean considerably authoritarian; relying on the same masculine mythos. A decisive masculine leader who can be relied upon to make the right call at the right time. Men like Abraham, Moses, David, Solomon found their analogs in Rockefeller, Carnegie, Ford, and Vanderbilt. Whatever the cause, neoliberalism found an ally in Evangelicals and they became mutually reinforcing ideologies. A not-so-fun game is to name any US-backed dictatorship of the last 50 years then take a look at the despot's policies. Ten out of ten times you'll find them to be neoliberal in nature and supported by the largest Evangelical church in the area.

Unsurprisingly, neoliberalism hit poor Evangelicals hard. Americans have always been defined by their ability to ignore barriers. Steinbeck once said, "The poor see themselves not as an exploited proletariat but as temporarily embarrassed millionaires." Admirable, that good ol' American "pull yourself up by the bootstraps" pluck. Alas, this mentality, a gross overestimation at the best of times, was downright destructive with the introduction of neoliberalism.

Evangelicals married the belief that God intervenes on behalf of the faithful with the mythology of the American Dream. Toss in the age-old Protestant love of work and an extreme stigma around poverty is created. It is shameful to be poor, an outward sign of moral lapse. When the rich Evangelicals say, "I owe it all to God," how are the impoverished to interpret the inverse? Likewise, when wealth and power are viewed as rightful rewards for hard work or even gifts from on high, exploitation and subjugation can't even enter the picture. Public opprobrium, American mythology, and Evangelical Prosperity Gospel all demand that the poor reinvent the cause of their poverty. If the wealthy obtained their riches through honest hard work, so could they. They could be millionaires or at least upper middle class if not for unfair hurdles like affirmative action, immigration, socialism, or some Jewish conspiracy. Whatever demagogue upholds the construct of the American dream while quoting scripture and regurgitating a scapegoat rationality will suddenly find himself a "man of the people." After all, the American dream requires the ability for people to transcend poverty with cleverness and hard work. Logically if they are working hard each day but are still somehow poor, then they must be either inept, dumb, or both. That's an identity no one would choose for themselves, especially if someone rich and successful offers them easy answers.

Neoliberalism, with the backdrop of Cold-War propaganda, has pulled another nasty trick on the Evangelical right with their fundamentalist view of gender roles. A world where it is a woman's God-ordained role to stay home, raise children, and see to domestic affairs. One where a man is to be the breadwinner and protector who can also fix things after working in the yard if he doesn't have a male child to do that for him. Ironically, they now denounce the very economic reforms that would allow for such a world, one where the average household could once again survive on a single income, as deadly socialism.

Traditional gender roles became a significant focus for Evangelicals from the 50s onwards. In no small part thanks to the foundation laid by Evangelical pastors and theologians like Mr Schaeffer and before him the legendary Billy Sunday. They made it abundantly clear that the woes of society stemmed from America's departure from biblical standards. Billy Sunday lamented back in 1916, "The Lord save us from – effeminate, ossified, three-carat Christianity."

A return to biblical standards was essential but not always

agreed upon. What did a Christian man or woman look like? In an era of trumped-up patriotism and demonization of Soviet egalitarianism, Jesus proved to be less than a good example. Turn the other cheek? Not very American. Thankfully the Bible does offer other more palatable options.

The Old Testament is awash with awful commandments from which to cherry-pick. Paul's opinion of women is less than charitable and offers plenty of fodder as well. With a few Bible verses in their quiver, pastors manned the pulpit ready to do battle. Sermons took up a militant tone, and countless books about raising girls to be girls and boys to be boys were written. All to halt the destruction of godly families and the wussification of Christianity. The ideal Evangelical man began to look less and less like the Biblical Jesus. Men were allowed to be genial, witty, even well-read, but behind all of it must be the potential for violence. Decisive and in charge, Christian men were to be leaders. In conjunction, Christian women were to be followers.

A militant masculinity took hold of the Evangelical mind. Patriotism, strength, and the capacity for violence were qualities to be fostered above all others.

Hints that Evangelicals would soon fully adopt violent patriotism pop up throughout its history. Mentor to Jerry Falwell, B.R. Lankin spent his early years traveling the Smokey Mountains on a mule, stopping to preach in remote towns. Said to have converted over 100,000 souls and reached millions more, Mr Lankin's igneous fundamentalism gained him notoriety and greatly influenced his protégé who named him the "prince of preachers". As a testament to Lankin's lasting influence, Falwell named the department of religion at Liberty University after him and had him buried on Liberty University grounds. Sermons like "America's Greatest Need" put Lankin in the good graces of the political establishment. Congressman William Jennings Bryan Dorn of South Carolina read this sermon into the congressional record on October 3, 1968. A quick glance at the sermon's context sheds a little light on Jerry Falwell's development:

In these days of national strife and international confusion, when the seeds of hatred are being cultivated in the hotbeds of communism and radicalism, let us throw back our shoulders, double up our fists, rough with the calluses of honest toil, and stand up for true, fundamental, godly Americanism. The Bible teaches patriotism, and patriotism was the light that burned in the hearts of the faithful in the midnight gloom of the dark ages.

And those are only the first two sentences. Godly Americanism was more than merely loving your country. It was accepting a rigid hierarchy into your personal life and in society at large. Men being in charge was key.

Billy Graham did his part to exemplify patriarchy as William Martin touched upon in his biography, *A Prophet with Honor: The Billy Graham Story*. Ruth, Billy's wife, apparently had aspirations of her own, but when they came into conflict with Billy's global evangelism circuit he was quick to remind her that the Bible dictates that "the husband is the head of the wife." A daughter of missionaries and a strong believer in biblical inerrancy herself, Ruth had no choice but to agree when Billy said, "I'll do the leading and you do the following."

The roles of men and women needed to be instilled young. Christian literature has always had an emphasis on child-rearing. I have already touched on the toxic masculinity promoted in *Bringing up Boys*, by James Dobson. A predecessor to Mr Dobson's book was a book called *How to Rear Children* by the influential fundamentalist pastor Jack Hyles. The chapter entitled "How to Make a Man out of a Boy" offers these nuggets of wisdom, "Teach him to be around boys that dress like boys. Teach him it is not Scriptural for a boy or man to have long hair or effeminate tastes in clothing." It gets much worse:

> Teach him to want to win.... We have bragged on good
> losers until our boys have received more rewards for losing
> gracefully than winning properly. The result has been that
> we now have a nation of young people who do not want to
> fight for their country and who are willing to let the strongest
> nation on earth bow down in shame before a little nation like
> North Vietnam. It is tragic, but true, that I know hundreds of
> men who couldn't beat their wives at Chinese checkers.

Why men should instinctively be better at Chinese checkers is
never explained.

Thankfully, what is explained is that a boy becoming a man is
dependent upon attending a church with a "masculine pastor,"
not being indoors very much, learning to fight, and importantly,
owning a gun. Really, the whole book reads like a transcript
from one of McCarthy's wet dreams. Perhaps not McCarthy's,
not enough gay sex. Toxic masculinity did not simply pop up
out of nowhere and the Evangelical adoption of it didn't either.
With every revolution comes a counter-revolution, and the
liberation movements of the 1960s were no exception.

Feminism was a blatant attack on the sacred social hierarchy
as ordained by Jesus himself. Or so fundamentalists loudly
proclaim to this day. Evangelical women were often co-
conspirators in maintaining their own subjugation. When
feminists like Betty Friedman pushed the novel idea that women
may want to be something other than housewives, she faced a
backlash from many Evangelical women. Some of whom may
have inwardly agreed, but were already too committed to allow
themselves to dream. The options left to many of these married
women were to risk tearing apart their families or maintain the
status quo. Women like Carmen Pate, Marabel Morgan, Phyllis
Schlafly, Beverly LaHaye, and later Debi Pearl offered these

women an out.

True liberation could not be attained through feminism; it could only be attained through submission to God via submission to your husband. Marabel Morgan wrote a book in 1973 that went on to sell over 10 million copies (twice as many as this book) entitled *The Total Woman*. The book entreats women to become sex slaves for their husbands and gives useful tips on how to best please them. Ideas like, "thrill him at the front door" in "A frilly new nightie and heels" or "nothing but saran wrap" precede darker instructions like:

It is only when a woman surrenders her life to her husband, reveres and worships him, and is willing to serve him, that she becomes really beautiful to him. She becomes a priceless jewel, the glory of femininity, his queen!

Beverly LaHaye, the wife of the aforementioned revenge-porn connoisseur Timothy LaHaye, co-authored a book with her husband called *The Act of Marriage*. A book I discovered at the age of 13 while snooping for Christmas presents in my parents' top dresser drawer. At the time it was the closest thing I had ever come to pornography, and I returned to its titillating pages several times for its graphic descriptions of sexual acts and positions. I did not come back for its casual dismissal of marital rape or its command for women to be "sexually responsive" to all their husbands' desires.

With the collapse of the Soviet Union came a discontinuity in American Evangelicalism. As John Eldredge wrote in *Wild at Heart*, "every man longs for a battle to fight" and it looked as if America had finally won not only the battle but the war. Evangelical masculinity floundered slightly in this time. More genteel interpretations of what it meant to be a biblical male enjoyed brief moments in the limelight. Tragically, the deep-rooted beliefs that the world was out to get them prevailed once again. Disturbed by the apparent feminization of American men, Evangelical leaders reminded their flocks of all the dangers only manly men could be prepared to face. Together with right-wing radio, Evangelicals pumped nitrous directly into the arteries of the culture wars. A superfluity of books lauding male chauvinism, militancy, and an almost homoerotic ruggedness hit the shelves. Authors like Dobson, Eldredge, Mark Driscoll, and John Piper all implore a return to some golden era of Christian masculinity. It doesn't take much reading between the lines for one to see that their idea of gold is actually lead. When fundamentalists flew passenger jets into the twin towers, Evangelical leaders had already adopted this new super-jacked, testosterone-soaked Jesus. Now it was time to deploy him. Islam, always considered the enemy by Evangelicals, was a ready-made replacement for the defunct USSR. Evangelicals approved of Bible verses being printed onto the assault rifles carried into Afghanistan and Iraq. I personally heard people in my church express their hopes that soldiers would follow in General Pershing's footsteps and dip ammunition in pigs' blood. That General Pershing did no such thing was a mere triviality. Propagating a made-up story without so much as questioning its validity, also kind of an Evangelical thing.

Militant, angry, and nationalistic Evangelicals preached sermon after sermon bolstering their perception of biblical maleness. The once prominent conviction of "everyday Christianity" was quickly replaced with "the ends justify the means." The ends being a protection and expansion of Christendom, and the means being murder, torture, and general savagery. Gallup and Pew polls showed Evangelicals supported torturing detainees and the death penalty by a wide margin in 2003 and 2004. Evangelical leaders like Chuck Swindoll would take to their respective radio shows and praise Bush for his invasion of Afghanistan and Iraq. In August 2004 Chuck prayed, "Our Father, I ask you to forgive us for the softness that has begun to characterize a generation." His prayer came after complaining about the liberal perception of Bush. "Our president is seen as a gun-toting, trigger-happy cowboy – are you kidding? I admire his restraint. He could have turned most countries into parking lots with the kind of firepower we have."

Undue deference for male leadership and hierarchies was simply accepted as mere orthodoxy. Perhaps one of the most widely read Evangelical authors of the time was John Piper. His writings lined the walls of my church's library and parents' bookshelf. Through his writings and sermons, he cultivated a dogma with sexist gender roles at its epicenter. John Piper, clarifying his earlier preaching at the "Desiring God 2012 Conference for Pastors," declared, "He [Jesus] has ordained for the church a masculine ministry." While being extremely careful to disavow authoritarianism, as Schaeffer with theocracy, it's hard not to get a sense he wishes for a world run by "biblically" authoritarian men. Perhaps his answer to a Q&A on episode 661 of his podcast best clarifies his stance on gender roles. The question posited was, "Should women be police officers?":

> Here is my conviction. To the degree that a woman's influence over a man, guidance of a man, leadership of a man, is personal and a directive, it will generally offend a man's good, God-given sense of responsibility and leadership, and thus controvert God's created order.

He did later clarify that it was ok for women to be civil engineers who discreetly direct men by developing roads or bridges. The problem lies in women personally directing men in any way.

> If a woman's job involves a good deal of directives toward men, they will need to be non-personal in general, or men and women won't flourish in the long run in that relationship without compromising profound biblical and psychological

issues. And conversely, if a woman's relationship to a man is very personal, then the way she offers guidance and influence will need to be more non-directive. And my own view is that there are some roles in society that will strain godly manhood and womanhood to the breaking point.

Piper calls himself a "complementarian," as in men and women have different gifts which complement one another, neither is better or worse. In reality, he advocates a strict hierarchy with men calling the shots.

One afternoon, a friend who went to an even more fundamentalist church than I did came over with a book used at her church for the "marrieds" Bible study. She kept the book, and years later when we were flat mates and fellow apostates, we would often read excerpts to each other while incredibly drunk. The book was called *Created to Be His Help Meet*, by Debi Pearl. Never reaching the popularity of *The Total Woman*, yet far surpassing it in sheer grossness, the book still sold over half a million copies. The thing most likely responsible for holding back Debi's success was that the book was written in 2004 but belonged in 1504. Hilariously euphemistic sex advice can be found throughout. Lines like "keep him drained at home, so he won't have any sexual need at work" and "Plan on a different addition to your 'birthday suit' each week" kept my friends and I in tears over shots of tequila.

Debi's idea of a godly woman is one that gives extreme deference to her husband, the church, and the government. She sets up a clear pattern in the book. Women are to blame for everything. I'm not being over the top here, they are to blame for literally everything, and men can only be judged by other men higher up the chain of command or by God. Here she blames Bathsheba for David murdering her husband:

Because Bathsheba was indiscreet, she caused great calamity, resulting in the bloodshed and suffering of many. Her lack of discretion cost her husband his life, his comrades-in-arms their lives, her baby son his life, and the integrity of one whom God upheld as a man after his own heart.

Debi also sets up marriages to be Petri dishes for abuse.

God does not step in and divest a father of his authority when he proves to be short-tempered and neglects his children, or when he is excessive ir his corporal punishment – Children are still required to obey an unreasonable and surly father. Likewise, wives are to obey unreasonable and surly husbands.

The last section of the book is dedicated to answering questions women have written to her. This part is truly heartbreaking. Many of these women require years of counseling and a good divorce lawyer. What Debi gives instead is brutal tongue lashings and heaps of guilt. One poor wife writes in not knowing what to do; she is distraught that her husband regularly demands sexual acts that she is not comfortable with. Debi knee caps the woman with:

When you married you signed over to become a minister to his needs. Your life's work is to minister to your husband. Marriage means becoming one flesh. It does not mean being best friends – it is your God-ordained ministry to your husband to be his totally enthusiastic sex partner, ready to enjoy him at all times. If you love your husband as God commands, you will always seek to give him pleasure. In so doing, you will fulfill your role as his suitable helper.

Another woman writes that she is concerned her husband allows the children to watch inappropriate television and movies. Debi, graceful and even-tempered as always, informs her reader that, "The Devil would love to steal your children's souls. He will not do it through your husband's TV; he will do it through your dishonor." To be both fair and balanced, she does suggest that a husband's punishment of children and wives should not cross the line of breaking any "just laws of the land." Even her caveat has a caveat.

From Piper to Pearl, these Evangelicals endorsed a toxic version of masculinity as the only biblical interpretation. They also promoted systems of power that were hotbeds for corruption and abuse. Like New Tribes Mission, these pastors and Evangelical "thinkers" set up institutions and churches with authoritarian male heads who were often considered above reproach. Unaccountable power led to similar results faced by the televangelists. Pastor after pastor was found guilty of abuse.

The formula is maintained today. The more authoritarian the pastor and the more they embrace a "biblical" masculinity, the more likely they are to be abusive predators. What's more, these men will be regularly shielded, as long as possible, from accountability by other believers in "biblical" masculinity.

Mars Hill superstar and manly man Mark Driscoll championed a warrior Christ who looked and acted nothing like the modern "Richard Simmons, hippie, queer Christ," who is a "neutered and limp-wristed popular Sky Fairy of pop culture that...would never talk about sin or send anyone to hell." He had landed himself in hot water several times for "chauvinistic, abusive and misogynistic" behavior. Ironically it wasn't Driscoll's machismo that finally got him in trouble in 2014.

We live in a completely pussified nation. We could get every man, real man as opposed to pussified James Dobson knock-off crying Promise Keeping homoerotic worship loving mama's boy sensitive emasculated neutered exact male replica evangellyfish, and have a conference in a phone booth.

Statements like this were not quite enough to get him fired. Nor was his blaming women for their unfaithful husbands' infidelity. When he was finally ousted it was for mishandling church money. Mars Hill dissolved shortly after his departure.

A lesser-known pastor who "ministered" near my home town, Mike Hintz, gained some notoriety in 2004 when presidential candidate George W. Bush pulled Mike up on stage with him while on the campaign trail. The presidential hopeful must have read up on Mike's crusade against modernity. Mike was a vocal proponent of "traditional family values," gender roles, and purity culture, even putting his name to a full page ad in the *Omaha World Herald* that demanded a complete ban on the sale of pornography. He urged teens to "avoid pursuing romantic relationships in favor of getting closer to God." That advice went for all teenagers except for the one he was sleeping with. When his affair with a 17 year old girl leaked he initially considered faking his own death and moving to Peru. Reconsidering, Mike turned himself over to the police a month after Bush won the presidency. Mr Hintz was convicted of three misdemeanor counts of sexual exploitation by a counselor and put on the sex offender list for ten years. Mike was interviewed on the podcast *An Open Letter* in 2017 where he briefly describes the event. Admitting to harming his wife and his family, he completely glosses over any trauma suffered by a 17 year old girl whose only mistake was trusting her youth pastor.

Southern Baptist leader and former seminary head Paige Patterson preached extensively on God-ordained gender differences which highlighted "biblical" misogyny. In 2014, he gave a sermon that came back to haunt him 2 years later. In it he describes a situation where he found himself with a young man and woman when a "nice" 16-year-old girl sauntered by.

The young man exclaims, "Man, is she built!" The other woman scolds him for his coarseness. Patterson then said he told her, "Ma'am, leave him alone. He's just being biblical." Patterson would later apologize for the sermon. However, Patterson continues to refuse to apologize for telling a rape victim not to go to the police but instead to forgive the man or to apologize for decades of sexist rhetoric. After heavily promoting Patterson's preachings, the SBC did an about face and forced him into retirement in 2018. They gave him a free place to live and will continue to pay him until he dies.

Megachurch pastor Bill Hybels was allowed to retire after too many allegations of unwanted sexual contact were brought against him in 2018. In 2014, homeschooling advocate and Christian curriculum creator Bill Gothard of Basic Life Principles (BLP) finally stepped down after 18 women came forward, many of whom were underage, accusing him of sexual assault. BLP also stands accused of covering for Gothard.

Dozens of denominations and thousands of churches across the country have been found guilty of covering up sexual misconduct within their ranks. A common factor has always been victim blaming. Perhaps the most consummate example springs from an investigation of sexual abuse at Bob Jones University in 2014. After telling police he had been abused, a young man was blamed by a BJU official for "tearing his family apart" and then told, "you love yourself more than you love God." My experience and research has led me to believe that abuse and cover ups in the Evangelical community rivals, if not surpasses, that of the Catholic church.

Talk about a bushel of bad apples. I believe there is even a Bible verse about a corrupt tree and evil fruit. The previous paragraphs offer a miniscule sampling of the rotten fruit on display. The Evangelical adoption of authoritarianism, chauvinism, and sexist theology not only turned their churches into playgrounds for power hungry abusers, but also made their congregants and communities into co-conspirators. If you believed, as Debi Pearl or Mark Driscoll do, that Christian men may be faulty but that they are God's representatives on Earth and that women are inherently deceptive, how much weight would you give to a woman who came forward? If the victim was a boy and the abuser a man, then the Devil must be in play and who better to confront the Devil than the church? When the secular world is trying every day to destroy God's people, why would you go to them for help? The pastor was put there by God himself, surely he knows what is best.

The far right was onboard with the Evangelical emphasis on machismo, militantism, and authoritarianism. They also couldn't agree more that the ends do in fact justify the means. The closeness shared between Christianity and the far right is not exactly new. Throughout the twentieth century you could replace "facsist" with "Christian right" around the world and not be too far off the mark. Salazar, Engelbert Dollfuss, Ante Pavelić, Jozef Tiso, Leon Rupnik, Franco, and even a hesitant Benito Mussolini are among the most famous, but the list can continue ad nauseum. Since Constantine, Christianity has courted authoritarianism, but in America, Christian nationalism was relegated to the fringe of society directly following the Second World War. As we've seen, that changed over time. The shift from fringe to mainstream was an incremental process, but anyone who has ever attended a Trump rally has seen that process nearing completion.

Chapter 10

Transitions

Boners arrived in 8th grade, and there was no one to tell me what was happening. My family had held me back from the "sex talk" part of 5th grade, so I learned about deodorant, but when the time came to talk about what might happen to our bodies soon I was in the hall. I remember asking my mom in sixth grade what sex was because I'd heard some people talking about it on our ever-droning Christian radio station and it sounded bad. "Don't worry about it," she said. Naturally, homeschooling did not come with a sex-ed class, but my Evangelical parents proudly presented me with a book called "60 Things God Said About Sex." Surprise! You guessed it! None of them were about sex. I still had no idea what sex was.

When 10th grade health class finally came around and I learned about sex from an educator, it was such a relief. But it didn't help normalize my experience. I was ashamed of my daily masturbations, as well as my very normal attractions to the opposite sex. Every day, I thought I was thinking and doing something wrong — something wicked. I prayed and prayed for God to stop my sin, and every week I confessed my failures to my men's accountability group. Turns out, the hormones "God" gave me were leading me to hell. I would walk the halls of my high school and notice girls, but would feel ashamed for how I would notice them, and for that reason did not feel confident prioritizing connections with them that were more than casual acquaintances or friendship.

I was not encouraged to grow up. If anything, I was the quintessential late-bloomer. I didn't have a driver's license until 17 or a job until college. And when it came to women, I had no game. Much of my sense of identity was tied up in my virginity and my purity. I got through all of high school and 4 years of college without even so much as kissing a girl on the lips, though

I accumulated a myriad of wonderful gal-pals. When it finally happened, I was 22. It turned out kissing was really fun. WHAT! I wasn't sure why I'd waited so long – it didn't seem like a big deal. I still hadn't dated, though. I had no idea what dating even entailed. I was 23 when I finally met a woman who was interested enough to pull me out of my shell. Her name was Aly. She was older than me, had no religious background, and we were mesmerized by each other. We could not have been more opposite. We started to date, but I insisted on maintaining my virginity – much to her disappointment. I would try new things, though. Allow compromises. I didn't know many other virgins at that point; they all married young. Laying in bed and touching each other felt pretty amazing.

We went to a fun Halloween party together that was a big event at a creative agency sponsored by Red Bull. Afterward, that night, I finally conceded and decided to "go inside." If you've had sex, I don't have to describe to you what that first spectacular moment was like. If you haven't yet, well, you have a lot to look forward to. But on the morning of November 1st I woke up distraught. I'd given away a core piece of my identity. I would and could never again be a virgin. I would never be able to "give" my virginity to someone, my untarnished self. My shame returned, and reinforced by a hangover, led me to some pretty grim feelings about myself. Was God disappointed? I didn't get a formal response to that, but Aly certainly was. Because she loved me, Aly felt hurt by my standoffishness and dark perspective after making a point of connection that had meant so much to her after 3 months of waiting patiently. It had felt good, and I had wanted it. I should have been happy, but instead I felt worthless, like a bedraggled puppy.
Mike, Nebraska

Graduation came and went and as I predicted not a whole lot had changed in my mind. All of my friends were in college or heading that way. The whole thing felt wrong to me. I did not like conformity, or the idea that life had universal steps which everyone must take. College was the most blatant form of conformity I could think of. It is laughable that I refused to look at my religion in the same light. I say "my religion" because I managed to look at all the others, including only slightly divergent Christian denominations, that way. How dumb Catholics must be to accept the word of a Pope as infallible. Mormons die and get their own planet? Jews die and get nothing? C'mon guys, use your brains!

College was not going to happen for me. I arrogantly believed myself to be too smart for it. Besides, college was a liberal hellscape which offered little in the way of a real education. Bible school had too many rules governing interactions with girls for me to commit to going there either. I had several girlfriends by this time and was certain there was not much else of importance going on in Lincoln, Nebraska. There was a growing need in me, one that must have been planted somewhere deep in my childhood and germinated with graduation. The need for movement and chaos. I could hear the distant howl of wind through a ship's rigging. I could feel the rhythmic jolts of an overcrowded and poorly maintained train as it chugged across a foreign landscape. I could taste the smoke of cigarettes shared with fellow vagabonds. I would stay up late at night marinating in sappy romantic imaginings where I wandered in strange lands and explored the ruins of lost civilizations.

I was dating a girl named Rebekah. We shared a desire to sail away into the unknown. However, she needed a spiritual goal attached to her adventures. I had adopted a mindset that I would best serve the kingdom by living a life so visibly otherworldly that the stranger would have to stop and ask me about it. I would free myself of materialism and earthly ties and wander the globe sharing the love of Jesus via raw spirituality and possibly sex if anyone was interested.

My Evangelicalism had taken on an outward appearance of

bland self-serving spiritualism. Inwardly it remained at the back of my mind silently spiteful and vindictive, unable to let go of either its conservative political stances or dogmatic clutch to guilt. Rebekah broke up with me using the perfectly acceptable explanation of, "you're distracting me from God." She then paid a lot of money to join the crew of a YWAM sailboat tasked with ministering to dolphins, or seafaring peoples, I can't remember.

I made up my mind that no matter what else was going on in my life, I would set out on adventure as soon as I had the money. I got a full-time job working in a boys group home. It was a grown-up job with a 401(k) and everything. I also picked up a job at the Henry Doorly Zoo in Omaha, working in their overnight education program. The job was a dream come true. Despite my early proclivity to hunt endangered crocodiles, I always had a love of animals. I soaked up every odd fact and interesting tidbit I could. I only worked weekends and was paid to talk about the things I loved best. Many nights, after my designated group of children and parents were asleep, I would walk the never silent zoo in the dark. The smell of hay and a wide variety of dung greeted my nostrils. I would watch the big cats sleeping or an addax keeping watch by the light of dim yellow bulbs. This bubble of the exotic only furthered my desire to leave.

I worked around 70 hours a week, but I wasn't saving money fast enough with bills and rent I found that I qualified for a medical study investigating a novel delivery method for morphine. Importantly, it paid 6k if you were selected to participate. I was accepted into the study and stayed the next 2 weeks in a blissful morphine-induced haze. They administered a drug to counteract the addictive nature of the morphine, but still, it was the easiest money I had ever made.

My resolve to escape Lincoln was only intensified by the hermetically sealed bubble in which I existed. Things that would have made headlines elsewhere were barely given a second glance here. While saving up to leave the country, I volunteered my Tuesday mornings to an Evangelical youth outreach program called Campus Life. Around ten of us would meet at a nearby middle school where we would play games with a bunch of kids then teach a Bible lesson. Campus Life is a national organization with over 1000 locations and has been disseminating Evangelicalism inside American public schools for 65 years. The chapter I was part of was headed by a very excitable, well-intentioned fellow named Nathan. As with many Christian nonprofit organizations, Campus Life put an unreasonably heavy workload on their employees without providing enough resources or oversight. On top of that, they then asked employees to fundraise for the majority of their salaries. This practice led to several less than optimal outcomes.

Outside of Tuesday mornings, we would also have weekend events with as many kids from school who opted to come. Most of these events were fun things like talent shows or trips to amusement parks. However, many of them were intended to ensure the message of God was firmly nailed in. It was at such a weekend event that Nathan came up with the perfect symbology for Christ's redeeming love. He usually kept his plans close to the vest, so I was as much along for the ride as the students I was supervising.

The evening had begun as usual with rowdy games followed by a dance-off. I was aware that tonight there was a more serious message planned, so I helped settle the group down to prepare for Nathan to start sharing. The message was on-brand, generic Evangelical fare. "We all have done things we are not proud of, but the good news is that Jesus can forgive anyone who asks." What came next was also nothing out of the ordinary. All the kids were instructed to write down whatever it was that they were ashamed of doing or what "burdens" they carried, onto a sheet of paper, then fold it up and put it in a basket. I had seen this all before. What I had not seen before was waiting for us outside. Nathan indicated we were to lead all the kids through the chilly night air and to the fire pit outside the building, where flames licked the air invitingly. There, a few feet from the pit, stood a newly erected 6-foot cross. Once all the kids were seated, Nathan proceeded to take each folded paper out of the basket and nail them to the cross. Explaining that, "When Jesus was nailed to the cross, he took all our sins upon himself, and when he died he took our sins to hell." A bit dramatic to be sure, but the usually rambunctious students were uncharacteristically silent. Nathan then picked up a cup of water from next to where he had been sitting and poured it over the top and down the cross's arms. "Perhaps to demonstrate the cleansing of our sins?" I thought to myself. Putting the cup back down, he pulled a burning stick out of the fire and touched it to the cross. Immediately it burst into flames. "Hooooooooooly fuck." The words I had hoped were contained within my head had escaped my lips in an elongated whisper. My throat became suddenly dry as I attempted to voice my concern, "Uh, Nate?" Clearly irritated by the interruption, he shot me a glance. Something in my wide-eyed stare must have shook loose whatever it had been that kept him from seeing the obvious because his countenance completely changed. He quickly shot the burning cross an apprehensive glance then rapidly surveyed the slack-jawed middle-schoolers. And that was the first and only cross burning I have ever attended.

I had purchased a ticket to Hanoi 6 months before my planned departure. The airline ticket was bought with credit card points using a scheme I thought up while working an overnight shift at the boys home. I was watching TV when an infomercial by the US Mint came on. They were advertising the new line of dollar coins featuring various presidents. The part that caught my attention was that they were offering free shipping and purchasing at cost. In other words, buy a dollar with a dollar, and they'd send it to you for free. I immediately got on the computer and went to the US Mint's website. I was checking to see if it allowed for a purchase using a credit card. It did. No way would this work. I purchased $100 of the coins with my credit card and waited. A few days later a hefty package arrived at my door. I immediately took it to the bank and deposited it without a hitch. I was downright giddy.

I did some quick research and found a list of credit cards with the best introductory offers and point plans. Several had deals like "receive $200 cashback after spending $2000" and "5X points for airfare." I ordered the best two that I qualified for and waited. When they arrived the next week I went back online and ordered $5000 of coins on each. Instantly making $500 cashback and more than enough points to purchase my flight to Vietnam. The coins came in the mail, I deposited them in the bank, and repeated the process several more times. Apparently, I was not the only person to recognize the value of that particular scam because the mint changed their policies only a few months after I had found out about it. Thankfully not before I had made about $3000 in cashback deals, enough points to buy a heap of useful gadgets, and my plane tickets.

No small part of the decision to finally buy the tickets came as a result of a girl I had met earlier that year departing for southeast Asia to teach. I do not believe I intended to chase Allie, but she was the inspiration and catalyst which finally got me on my way. From the beginning of our relationship I knew she would be leaving. That suited us both just fine. What didn't sit well with me was that while Allie embarked on something huge and unknown, I festered in Lincoln, Nebraska.

I cannot pinpoint exactly when I stopped regularly attending church, but without the weekly booster shot of sexual repression my inhibitions were quickly burned up in a feverish demand for physical expression. We had only been seeing each other for a few months, but together, Allie and I destroyed decades of shared repression. Like me, she had grown up an Evangelical and was actively sorting out what she still believed. The intimacy necessary to shatter a pair of rose-colored glasses was never established between us and we could do no wrong the other was unwilling to overlook. Having only recently dismissed our moral qualms with fornication, we pursued the newfound frontiers of sex religiously.

We parted unceremoniously. I drove her to the airport and walked her to the security checkpoint. She kissed me goodbye, then passed into the hallowed grounds of the Transportation Security Administration without looking back. She rarely had a mind for the past, and maintained a sentimentalism only for her beloved books.

Going to Vietnam felt intuitive to me. I didn't belabor the decision or question the destination. Perhaps it was a lifetime of growing up on Stallone and Chuck Norris playing troubled Vietnam vets in the movies, but I had been drawn to Vietnam since I was a kid. Looking back I can see the waning in my Evangelical ardor was preceded and directly influenced by my waning belief in American exceptionalism. And nothing misses the mark of American exceptionalism like the Vietnam war.

"I know it sounds batshit crazy, but it's true! On my dead mother's grave, it's true!" The rangy passenger in the aisle seat pleaded emphatically. "They're all there in a small village close to the Chinese border. They wouldn't talk to me, but could you blame them?"

"Then how can you be so sure?" I asked, with a straight face.

"Three old white guys, two of which have several mixed kids, my age, all living in the same village. I asked around, and the locals who would say anything said the same thing. Long, long time, they said. And these locals were no fucking spring chickens themselves! So where the fuck else could they come from? Loung Lang, is only about – do you know kilometers? You never know with Americans."

"Yes, I know kilometers, but should I know Loung Lang?" I retorted.

"Oh, it's a pretty well-known POW camp. One of the first, I think, anyway it's only about 45 kilometers from where those guys live now and I have a friend, an ex-PLA colonel, who says he knows that a few POWs chose to remain in Vietnam when good ol' Uncle Sam turned his back on them." Donovan ran his sentences together with a growing excitement. He had a vigor shared by the infirmed and conspiracy theorists. I wondered how many other airline passengers had been assaulted by his intensity over the years, but I had to interrupt.

"Hold on a second," I said. "You think that after being captured and tortured, those guys just what? Decided to forgive and forget then shack up with a few Viet Cong?"

"Not everything you've heard on TV is true. The Chinese, but more importantly, the Russians had their eyes on some of those POWs. Especially any pilot or spook. A few of the high value types were passed back and forth across the border with China. If they cooperated they got treated better than Mao himself! Imagine being imprisoned by a sympathetic captor who was simply fighting for his homeland when your own country fucks you right up the ass. I mean Nixon knew there were far more than the 600 POWs! He fucking knew it! He also knew that the USSR would never let Hồ Chí Minh turn 'em over. So, Nixon agreed to the bullshit number the VC gave him and told the other 1000 or so POWs still in prisons all over Vietnam to kiss off! I'm sure he convinced himself it was better for America, or some horse shit but either way he royally screwed every last American that wasn't lucky enough to be in that 600."

Something seemed off with his history, but it made some sense. More importantly, it was exciting. I could feel this energetic Kiwi pulling me in, and I was not altogether unwilling. Fantastic imaginings swirled around in my head. An interview in a grass hut on stilts, the room filled with a blue-gray haze from countless cigarettes smoked by men who were not supposed to exist. Exposing decades of lies and betrayal by the US government. I had only met Donovan 4 hours earlier when my attempts to ignore him had failed. You can only put your earbuds back in so many times before it gets ridiculous. Now that he had a captive audience he was relentless.

"Fucking Boris Yeltsin himself said that the USSR had taken POWs from Vietnam. I mean really, that's proof enough, right? Good men were left to die by the very country they were fighting for," Donovan continued.

"Exactly!" I said, pulling away from my ponderings. "From what you've said, they are free now. Why don't they go home or at least spit in the eye of the people who betrayed them, and announce their existence? No one would simply forget about it and start a new life in the middle of nowhere, Vietnam."

"Maybe they were held for years after the war and all that reeducation actually worked, or they made a deal, or maybe the Vietnamese showed them a bit more hospitality than their fellow Americans would have. Being called a baby killer back in the good ol' US of A has a limited appeal. There were no parades, and no glory. Fuck, I don't know, but I sure as hell want to find out!" Donovan sank back into his seat and let out a long breath looking like he needed a cigarette. Instead, he took a sip of what had to be luke-warm tea, and set it back on the tray table in front of him. I looked at this too-thin man with a good deal of skepticism. His light gray eyes seemed to stare through the curved roof of the 757 and into the sky above. His spent energy settled into a stony resolve. I looked at him a moment longer before I reached under the seat in front of me and pulled out a pen and notebook. Knowing that this was probably a bad idea didn't stop me from asking how I could get ahold of him.

"Hard to say, I'm not exactly on the grid anymore," he told me flatly. I have long since learned to limit my interactions with anyone who speaks too often of "the grid." I make exceptions for electricians and the occasional hippy. This lesson had yet to be learned when I met Donovan. So, when he finally came up with a number that he could occasionally be reached at, I wrote it down and gave him my email address.

"I'll email you when I get to Phnom Penh," he said as he folded the paper and put it in his right breast pocket. I was unsure what that meant for someone "off the grid" and I was about to ask when he said, "If you're around, maybe you can meet my Chinese friend and we'll see what happens from there." I nodded, sensing an end to our conversation. With the departure of all that jittery energy he looked like a different person. Almost like a respectable businessman, not the shady huckster from earlier. It was as if with a sigh he had breathed out some kind of caffeinated demon to be recycled into the plane's air supply. However, when I looked at him in profile after he went back to examining the ceiling, I noticed a certain, indescribable glint. One that spoke of guile and mistrust. I leaned my chair back, to the chagrin of the passenger behind me, and closed my eyes. Maybe it was Donovan's half-crazed nature or the way his smile never reached his eyes, but something about him felt dangerous. Not violent exactly, his scrawny frame and skeletal hands did not belong to a violent man, but he was unsafe. Like an old Stalinist bureaucrat who ordered countless killings but has never himself snuffed out a life.

"You a Christian?" he asked abruptly.

"Yeah."

"Figures," he said. "All you Americans are."

"Not really," I protested.

"You're not really a Christian?

"No, I mean not all Americans are Christians."

"Sure they are, look at your country. You can't even be in government if you're not a Christian. It's all a racket. Organized religion is how they control people.

"They?"

"The people at the top, the ones in charge, they're fucking reptiles. Not even human, they don't care about anything or anyone. Their fucking sadists and they run the show."

"Like, actual lizards?"

"No, like they're cold-blooded ass holes. I'm not fucking crazy. These people, and I mean like real important people, get off on control and sadism. I've met a few. They pull the strings. All the shit that hurts people, prison, poverty, hunger, not being able to go to the fucking hospital. It's by design. Each a string. Their biggest string is religion. Think about it. Your church, they supported invading Iraq and Afghanistan and probably every other war, didn't they?"

I said I didn't know, but I did know and Donovan was right. He launched back into his diatribe.

"I'm sure they did. That's what I am talking about! Religion is all about control."

The remainder of the flight was spent in silence. Until the wheels touched down in Taiwan. "I'll see you later," he said with a smile as if we were old friends. "Sure thing," I said routinely. He disembarked in Taipei. He had plans to fly to Thailand in a week but had business to take care of first. The crew allowed for anyone continuing on to Hanoi to stay onboard during the layover. Although I needed to stretch my legs after the 13-hour flight, I wasn't about to follow Donovan off the plane. He made his way to the front and out of my sight. I met up with Donovan and his PLA contact a couple of months later in Cambodia, but that's a tale for another time. I never found the fabled POWs.

It was a cloudy afternoon in July when I landed just north of Hanoi at the Nội Bài international airport. The country has seen several thousand of me every month since the turn of the century. Each incarnation believes himself to be distinctive and adventurous. Each hopes to discover what no one else has yet seen. Although no one could have persuaded me that I was the carbon copy of anything. I was entirely swallowed up in youthful naivete and a belief in my own exceptionalism.

The squat city of Hanoi was the storied home of the Viet Cong and the spring waters that once fed the communist flood to the south. The entire city seemed not to have a single building taller than ten stories. Its streets all tossed together in an afterthought and woven into the fabric of the ancient city haphazardly. My equally old taxi veered into a massive roundabout where the other vehicles appeared to have no idea which direction traffic was supposed to flow. As an American, I did not have as rich of a history with the roundabout as, say, your average European, but I was reasonably sure that one of its defining features was a uniform circular pattern of traffic. This was not the case here. Drivers would enter the roundabout then pursue the shortest route to their desired exit, causing a patchwork of cars, trucks, buses, and mopeds. This living knot of traffic writhed and pulsed until it spat us out three streets over from our entrance. My driver deftly navigated the seemingly unintelligible throng until he pulled up in front of a hostel in the Old Quarter. It had a balcony jutting out over a weathered plastic sign that read "Green Tree Backpackers Hotel and Hostel." Directly below the plastic sign, there was a much newer one that read "Lonely Planet's Top Pick."

Vietnam was absolutely everything I had dreamed of back in Lincoln. The cities were like nothing I had ever seen, with the most incredible food around every corner. Old women serving up broths of every color to patrons on plastic chairs. Men pushing carts of steamed pork buns or banh mi sandwiches. Roasted ducks and entire pigs hung on hooks in open windows. The people were a complex blend of kindness with a sharp, no-nonsense business acumen. One moment you could be invited into the home of a stranger and the next be harangued for not purchasing something you had only stopped for a second to admire. My evenings were spent drinking beers with strangers and conversing in pantomime. Then wandering for endless hours through narrow alleys lit by Chinese lanterns and flickering street lamps. The air filled with fragrant sandalwood smoke from the incense which burned in the crooks of trees and at the altars in hundreds of spirit houses. I was in heaven.

Vietnam, then all of southeast Asia, introduced me to many things that would forever alter the way I perceived the world. Almost upon touching down, my newly adopted spirituality abandoned me. Without any intention or desire, I traded everything I had known for this world of color and light. It was as if there simply was not enough room in me for both who I had been and who this place, this experience, made me want to be. Below my freewheeling enlightenment, the meticulously crafted Evangelical worldview which had been so deliberately instilled over the last two decades remained, but in torpor. Even dormant, my faith experienced the corrosive effects of experience.

For the first time since I left Youth Group, I found a community willing to accept me without hesitation. Backpackers get a bad rap, and often for good reason, but on the whole they're a great group of people. You'll recognize them by the uncut hair and unkempt clothes, not to mention the ubiquitous, oversized pack that takes up the entirety of the overhead compartment.

It was while sailing on a large Vietnamese Junk in Halong Bay that I first felt as if I belonged to a group, not through obligation, but by choice.

I could not help but be filled with a sense of awe and otherworldliness as I looked up at the limestone monoliths jutting hundreds of feet out of the water like sharks' teeth. Some are capped with green vegetation populated by monkeys, cuckoos, and sea eagles. The cliffs were riddled with caves housing hidden temples and shrines. Each morning a thick blanket of fog would envelope the boat, compounding the ethereal feel. The very last night of my 4-day voyage I was enjoying the company of friends I had made while at sea. A Spanish couple and two girls from London. We were passing around cigarettes and a bottle of wine on the observation deck.

I never became comfortable with calling them "fags," no matter how emphatically the Brits encouraged me. The deck slowly emptied of other guests, and by midnight only the four of us remained. We reclined on large cushions; the Spaniards were wrapped around each other in a single lounge chair. With eyes searching the stars, we shared a silence. The night resonated with wellbeing. I felt accepted by the four seasoned backpackers and through them by an eternal fraternity of wanderers. I was happy in a way that was very new to me.

I wandered through Vietnam and up the Mekong into Cambodia, my boat sinking along the way. Rescued by a passing longboat, I made my way to Phnom Penh. It was while exploring the city that I picked up a copy of *First They Killed My Father*. I was familiar with the Khmer Rouge, but the book laid bare the regime's recent horrors. Curiosity piqued, I went to the school turned prison where the regime tortured and experimented on prisoners. I read accounts of children "doctors" cutting open subjects and inserting rabbit pellets or replacing blood with unfiltered coconut milk. This place shook me and terrified me, but I felt compelled to continue on to the infamous killing fields.

There I saw the bone pagoda, a glass structure filled with the remains of 8000 victims — their skulls with the telltale cracks and holes of being murdered with blunt tools. A path led through the fields, and on either side there were massive shallow graves. At the front of the path was a stump worn smooth by thousands of skulls being crushed against it. I was told that if you were to scratch at the surface of the soil around the stump, you could still find hundreds of teeth. I took the dirt trail winding around the graves and to the back where a chain-link fence closed off the place from the outside. Right outside the fence were two small boys; one was maybe 10 and the other 5 or 6. Cambodia is filled with polyglot street children, each able to sell postcards, books, or trinkets in a dozen different languages. These two held nothing in their hands and their ill-fitting clothes were torn and threadbare. The older one said something to me in French, so I stepped closer to the fence. Reading my lack of understanding, he tried again in English. "You want us to suck you?" he said, pointing at himself then his younger companion. I stared at their tiny round faces in absolute horror. Surrounded by death, then confronted with this. It was too much. I stumbled backward, turned, and ran toward the entrance stopping only moments later to vomit into an excavated grave.

That night I could not sleep. I cried and demanded an explanation from the God I still believed in. For the first time I thought I might hate him. I for sure hated whatever white person had made those young boys think they'd be successful in propositioning me. I hated myself for being there. I felt somehow responsible for their condition. I felt cowardly and exploitive as if I had acquiesced.

The remainder of my travels through Cambodia had that early experience overshadowing them. I explored the ancient throne of the Angkor and slept in Ta Keo temple after hiding from security. I watched the moon rise over the ruins of a long-dead city – the stone faces of forgotten deities watching me from their permanent resting places. I woke in the morning to find a small cobra not far from my feet. I got my things together and started another day of explorations. You had to be careful not to tread too far from the beaten path in Cambodia. The country is littered with both unexploded ordnance from the illegal American bombardment during the Vietnam war and leftover landmines from the Khmer Rouge. The entire time I kept my mind firmly on the experience at hand, trying not to think too deeply about my inevitable crisis of faith.

Whenever and wherever possible I like to travel by ship or train. Something about them brings me back to a time in which I have never lived. I was on a train heading for the Malaysian border after having spent the last 80 days in Thailand when I met Phra Chamroon. I was standing on the back platform of the last train car watching the tracks disappear around a bend when a middle-aged monk in a mustard yellow robe joined me. He stood there for some time before he asked, "Do you have a cigarette?" in perfect English. I did and handed him one, lighting it between his teeth as he leaned forward.

"Thank you very much," he said after a deep exhalation of smoke.

"My pleasure. I'm Lance," I responded and stretched my hand out in greeting. He shook it and reiterated my name to make sure he had got it correct. He had. Introducing himself as Phra Chamroon with a small bow. He was a short man, even by Thai standards, with kind, round eyes and the customary shaved head. After some small talk about where I was from and if I liked Thailand or not, the conversation went where so many others had before and would go after. To religion. I discovered he was on his way to a ceremony where his rank in the monastery would be confirmed. Curious, I asked him what it was like being a monk and if there were a lot of religious rules he had to follow.

"Not too many, no. As a novice it is more difficult. When I was a novice I had a very hard time at first, but I was also very young and naughty." At this he giggled, causing me to smile in return.

"I like to eat when I like to eat, so yes that was hard. But the precepts are there to help teach us how best to live."

"I didn't know monks were allowed to smoke," I joked.

"And drink too!" he added with a full laugh. "It is not about what you can and cannot do, it is about the conscience, it is about the will. And in this way I have but one rule."

"What is that?" I asked with genuine interest.

"Only do what is beautiful."

I spent the next several years wandering across borders, just me and my large, green Atmos 50 backpack. That pack became my boon companion. It was with me on the back of a motorcycle through the monsoons of Vietnam. It was with me at the dusty ruins of the Angkor in Cambodia. It survived the hands of curious children for half a year while I taught second grade in Laos. It weathered dozens of rides on buses, boats, tuk-tuks, trains, and taxis in Thailand. It proved a decent pillow when I slept in the streets of Malaysia. It held the medical supplies I much needed in Fiji. My pack was tossed, rolled, dragged, and dropped while hitchhiking around New Zealand. It survived a cyclone and a 53-day voyage across the Pacific in a small sailboat. It kept the water out on the mist-soaked island of Chiloé. It saw the mighty Futaleufu River, mountains, and glaciers as it traversed Patagonia. It kept the desert sands of the Chaco out while in Paraguay. It was almost lost on the beaches of Florianopolis. It was squashed in the bottom of a dugout canoe for weeks as I explored the deep Amazon. It was my bunkmate in Colombia and Panama. It almost caught on fire on New Year's Eve in Costa Rica. It has been up and down the Andes, Smokies, Rockies, and Sierra Nevadas. It is still with me now.

Everywhere I traveled took a little from me but gave back something in return. I fluctuated from secret atheist to evangelizing Christian multiple times. I never spoke of my doubts to anyone. While hitchhiking around the north island of New Zealand, I was adopted by an international group of French, Canadian, Israeli, and Kiwi travelers. The ten of us were squished into a small van headed to some secret beach on the east coast by Wainui. After we had parked the van and hiked for about two-and-a-half hours, we arrived at a long crescent of white sand backed by ancient Tōtara trees. The waves crashed on the sand as the sun set, and we lit large bonfires along the beach. Drinking directly from several vodka and cognac bottles, we all stripped naked and jumped into the sea. The water was cold and the dip short-lived. Instead, we took to running up and down the beach and climbing the broad-limbed trees. Naked, I fell from one branch and hit another before crumpling to the sand. Two equally naked Canadian girls helped me to the fire where we dressed and shared a spliff with the French guys who owned the van.

"My favorite part of the Bible was when God gave man free will then drowned them all for using it!" said Hector in his heavily accented English. "No, No! It is when he killed himself to save us from himself!" interjected his friend only slightly more intelligibly. All three of the Frenchmen were intransigent atheists. How the discourse started remains foggy, but something in my subconscious regularly steered any conversation that lasted more than 5 minutes toward the religious. The topic had scared off the rest of the party, excepting one Kiwi bystander. Looking back, I think the Kiwi, a kindly girl named Christine, stayed behind to break up any confrontation should the need arise. "You actually believe there's some guy in the sky judging us?" Hector asked.

"Well, not exactly some guy in the sky, but yes," I replied, inhaling deeply on the spliff, wishing my high would return.

"I do not mean to offend you, but that is really stupid," Hector said again.

"Have you ever gone to church?"

"Why would I?"

"It is not that bad; there's a lot to be learned there. You might like it. You never know unless you try."

"I know I wouldn't like being fucked up the ass by a horse. I don't have to try to know that!"

"He's not saying he'd get fucked up the ass at church," Jules helpfully chimed in. "He's just saying he would not like church like he would not like a horse fucking him in the ass."

"I got that. Look, I don't think any less of you for not believing in God."

"Well, I think much less of you," Hector replied. I was a bit taken aback, I didn't feel insulted, but his blunt rebuke of Christianity was something I had never encountered. Even more than that, I felt as if I was arguing with myself, and hearing someone mirror my own thoughts and rebukes back at me served to shake a memory loose. I was back in a Panamanian river being surrounded by crocodiles and refusing to let go of a dead bird.

I left New Zealand 3 months later on a small sailboat headed for South America. Hit by a cyclone after only 5 days we were forced to return to shore for repairs. Setting out again a week later, the next 53 days were spent almost entirely in silence as neither the captain nor the first mate spoke much English. The time was measured in beautiful sunsets and equally beautiful sunrises complemented by night skies filled with stars. That was until we sailed far enough south that the sun no longer set but instead hovered in a perpetual twilight. The solitude of those weeks onboard helped me sift through thoughts I had pushed to the back of my mind. Most important was the decision to be less sure of what I thought I knew about the world.

Chapter 11

The Final Chapter

Being an Evangelical was like living inside of an abusive relationship. The ever-present threat of violence from the very person who is supposed to love you the most. Constantly being told how much the man with the cocked fist cares about you. I couldn't reconcile the love of Jesus with the eternal damnation that waited for anyone fool enough to reject his "free gift."
Amber, Oregon

I was working on restoring a marine refuge in Fiji when I got the news that Donald Trump was now the Republican candidate for president. His eventual election to the presidency hit me as a surprise, but I had expected his nomination after only a few weeks into the primary. He validated every imagined oppression and slight that Evangelicals had been bravely enduring for decades. False claims of oppression may not be among the fruits of the spirit, but they became the ripest apple on the Evangelical tree during the 2016 and 2020 campaigns. Donald Trump promised to be everything the Christian nationalists wanted and more. I hold that the majority of the 81 percent of Evangelicals who voted for the Donald did not hold their noses and do so, they held their Bibles. After all, Evangelicals had already been flocking in the tens of thousands to megachurches headed by sociopathic megalomaniacs for years.

In his typical Trumpian lyricism, Donald propounded Christian nationalism with every breath on the campaign trail. During a "speech" in 2016 to a group of Florida pastors, he said:

You know that Christianity and everything we're talking about today has had a very, very tough time. Very tough

154

time...We're going to bring [Christianity] back because it's a good thing. It's a good thing. They treated you like it was a bad thing, but it's a great thing.

In the same speech where he quoted "two Corinthians," he also babbled out this bit of barely intelligible Christian nationalism:

Christianity, it's under siege. I'm a Protestant. I'm very proud of it. Presbyterian to be exact. But I'm very proud of it, very, very proud of it. And we've gotta protect, because bad things are happening, very bad things are happening, and we don't – I don't know what it is – we don't band together, maybe. Other religions, frankly, they're banding together and they're using it. And here we have, if you look at this country, it's gotta be 70 percent, 75 percent, some people say even more, the power we have, somehow we have to unify. We have to band together...Our country has to do that around Christianity.

During a July 2020 interview with Fox News, Donald Trump claimed that if Biden won the election. "religion will be gone." Throughout his presidency, he blew on every Christian nationalist dog whistle that he or Steve Bannon could think of. Trump and his strategists believing that Christian nationalists represent the majority of Evangelicals doesn't make it so. The numbers do.

Clemson researcher and sociologist Andrew Whitehead along with University of Oklahoma sociologist Samuel Perry published a first of its kind deep dive into Christian nationalism in their book *Taking America Back for God* They set out to discover how prevalent Christian nationalism was in America. What they discovered shouldn't surprise you if you have read this far. Evangelicals are now, by a wide margin, Christian nationalists. Seventy-eight percent, to be exact. The book incorporates reputable quantitative surveys done over multiple years with thousands of people and in-depth qualitative interviews done by the authors. Their methodology is impeccable.

Defining Christian nationalism can be difficult. Whitehead and Perry use it "to describe an ideology that idealizes and advocates a fusion of American civic life with a particular type of Christian identity and culture." They are explicit in saying that Evangelicalism is not synonymous with Christian nationalism. And I agree with them; it doesn't have to be. I have read articles and books by Evangelicals who disdain Christian nationalism, but I have not met one recently. They isolate the definition further:

Christian nationalism is a cultural framework that blurs distinctions between Christian identity and American identity, viewing the two as closely related and seeking to enhance and preserve their union. It is undergirded by identification with a conservative political orientation (though not necessarily a political party), Bible belief, premillennial visions of moral decay, and divine sanction for conquest. Finally, its conception of morality centers exclusively on fidelity to religion and fidelity to the nation.

Calling people all over the country and asking if they are Christian nationalists would offer poor results. Instead, participants were asked if they strongly disagree, disagree, agree, or strongly agree with the following statements:

1. The federal government should declare the United States a Christian nation.
2. The federal government should advocate Christian values.
3. The federal government should enforce strict separation of church and state.

4. The federal government should allow the display of religious symbols in public spaces.
5. The success of the United States is part of God's plan.
6. The federal government should allow prayer in public schools.

Depending on how they responded to each statement they received scores from 0-24 (all strongly disagree = 0, all strongly agree = 24). Those scores placed them in 1 of 4 categories; "Rejecters, Resisters, Accommodators, or Ambassadors." The categories are pretty self-explanatory. To be a "rejector" you must have strongly disagreed with each statement. Rejecters make up 7 percent of America. "Resisters" score between 6-11 and make up 27 percent of the country. "Accommodators" scored between 12-17 and encompass 32.1 percent of Americans. Scoring between 18-24, "Ambassadors" make up a staggering 19.8 percent of the country. That is one-fifth of Americans that line up with far-right Christian nationalist ideals. Inside of Evangelicalism, the "Accommodators" make up 40 percent and the "Ambassadors" constitute 38 percent. Combining these two categories is where I personally group Christian nationalists inside of Evangelicalism. Whitehead and Perry essentially cut the "Accommodators" category in half and hold that roughly 50 percent of Evangelicals embrace Christian nationalism.

Whether it's 78 percent or 50 percent it's a massive blow to democracy. Christian nationalism is a form of fascism, and we have at least a fifth of the country who would love to see a Christian fascist regime in America. There is an old antifascist slogan from the 1930s: "Fascism means war." It is an excellent encapsulation of the facts. The dual meanings of "we will always fight fascism" and "war is the very nature of fascism" couldn't be better articulated. Not too dissimilar from German workers in the 1930s, America's workers have been the recipients of the worst kinds of austerity. The causes may be different but the results are similar enough. A disenfranchised and desperate working class.

Neoliberalism has deindustrialized huge swathes of America and rid the majority of the country of any semblance of job security. Real wages have diminished for the last 30 years, while costs of education, home ownership, entrepreneurship, and just about everything else have gone up. According to The Congressional Research Service, almost half of Americans live in poverty when real wages are accounted for. In 2016, Pew put together a Household Expenditures and Income survey that found that the poorest third of Americans spend half their income on housing alone. The disparity between rich and poor has reached record highs. Being poor has been virtually illegalized across the nation. Small wonder the United States, which has less than 5 percent of the world's population, now incarcerates about 25 percent of the world's prisoners. In light of such realities, Christian nationalists have seen their numbers swell. Yet, some Americans resist the notion that this sort of insidious fascism is festering in our suburbs and church halls.

I was called out for being too extreme on the night of November 3, 2020, for claiming that the election was really about Christian nationalism. When a landslide rejection of fascism failed to materialize, it no longer mattered who technically won the presidential election. One of the few ways to combat Christian nationalism is to ensure meaningful work is readily available and that living conditions are dramatically improved. Trump wasn't the disease, he was a symptom, and Joe Biden, while immeasurably less repugnant, is unlikely to abandon neoliberalism. Biden, a devout Catholic, does not appear to harbor strong Christian nationalist intent. His piety will not shield him from the one-fifth of people who may see him as an agent of the Devil. This is especially true as the old Evangelical tensions with Catholicism are resurfacing. Robert James Jeffress, pastor to over 140,000 Southern Baptists and whose Easter service Trump had attended remotely in 2020, is famous for his belief that the Catholic church was founded by Satan himself. Bob Jeffress went full "turning the frogs gay!" in a 2010 segment on his radio show *Pathway to Victory* when he claimed:

> The high priests of that fake religion, [Catholicism] that false religion, the high priests of that religion would wear crowns that resemble the heads of fish, that was in order to worship the fish-god Dagon, and on those crowns were written the words, "Keeper of the Bridge," the bridge between Satan and man.

America's civic religion has managed to obfuscate the immense threat posed by Christian nationalists. If the men and women who stormed the Capitol building, resulting in five deaths, were carrying Islamic flags while shouting "Allahu Akbar," everyone would know exactly what to call them. But when rioters hold their open palms up to heaven praising God in the evacuated chambers as a giant cross rests outside the breached gates, then suddenly everyone is confused. Ignore the countless cardboard placards with Bible verses scrawled on them. Ignore the Christian flags being waved by praying looters. Ignore that both historically and in the minds of the bearers, the Confederate battle flag stands for a Christian nation. Ignore the signs reading "Jesus saves," or "only God and Donald Trump can save America." Ignore the self-professed religious zeal of the rioters. Ignore everything and pretend those people were "just mad they lost." But know this, ignoring too many uncomfortable truths is exactly what got us here.

It's a dangerous feedback loop. Trump, like every despot before him, did not materialize out of thin air. The MAGA hats didn't grow the heads underneath them. Christian nationalists saw themselves reflected in Trump and put him in the White

House. Trump then fed them everything they wanted, causing their influence to grow. Trump could not have come to power without Christian nationalists, but the inverse is not exactly true. The underlying current in American polity that demanded a Trump-like figure has been swelling for years. To look at the people who amassed in DC the first week of 2021 as dupes or merely fanatical Trump supporters is to commit us to a never-ending game of whack-a-mole with wannabe Christian nationalist tyrants.

Religious freedom and democracy are not biblical principles, and only enjoy the protection of Christian nationalists as long as they can be manipulated in their favor. California megachurch pastor and best-selling author John F. MacArthur made this abundantly clear in a series of sermons he delivered in January 2021. After claiming on Sunday the 17th that the nation had "permanently" voted out integrity, truth, and righteousness when it voted out Donald Trump, he had this to say about the Biden administration:

> The new administration will uphold religious freedom? I don't even support religious freedom. Religious freedom is what sends people to hell. To say I support religious freedom is to say I support idolatry, it's to say I support lies, I support hell, I support the kingdom of darkness. You can't say that. No Christian with half a brain would say, "We support religious freedom." We support the truth!

Turns out the Danbury Baptists might have another letter to write. MacArthur chased this "quiet part out loud" sermon with an equally dismal one the following week:

> Now it may shock you. The Bible doesn't advocate democracy. The Bible doesn't mention democracy. The Bible doesn't comment on democracy. The Bible doesn't define democracy.

There is no place in all of the Bible where you even find democracy. There is no country revealed in Scripture where it existed; it is never affirmed by God.

He is right, of course. The Bible says nothing about democracy, or germ theory for that matter. What he is getting at is that democracy is unlikely to be God's ideal system of governance. Afterall, heaven is not governed by the will of the people and, if you believe as MacArthur does, that an omniscient personal God gave us his perfect Word, it would stand to reason that God would have at least mentioned democracy if it were worth mentioning at all. MacArthur goes on to seemingly endorse theocracy while simultaneously drubbing the Vatican for having one. I wish I could tell you that MacArthur is some fringe lunatic; however, he is easily considered one of the most influential pastors alive.

When I listen to the paranoid ramblings of Christian nationalists or Qanon acolytes, I hear echoes of my time in Youth Group. The relentless pressure to be appreciative of, and obsequious to, biblical hierarchies. The constant fear of spiritual warfare, which has now found a home in the deep state and demonic Democratic pedophiles. The unbending faith in vague prophecy, the distrust of "the world," the nativism, and the praise of inflexible thinking all smack of Evangelical flavor. I was a number in their ranks. As diligent a believer as they come. More than once I formed a prayer chain around the nearest abortion clinic, ambushed acquaintances for Jesus, and belittled dire injustices with the tagline "we're in a fallen world."

My time in Youth Group may pale in light of what's to come. Today's Evangelical youth culture has shifted dramatically further toward the Charismatic Dominionist end of the Evangelical spectrum. Events like "The Send," which numbered over 60,000 in 2019 and managed 140,000 in 2020, represent the future of Christian nationalism. The latest Send conference was held in Brazil mid-Covid outbreak and featured surprise guest Jair Bolsonaro, who was met with rapturous applause upon shouting "Brazil belongs to God!"

The Send has all the traditional trappings of Evangelical youth culture with the added pizzazz of magic. In 2019 and 2020, faith healings repaired concussions, broken bones, and removed hepatitis C with nothing more than a "hallelujah praise Jesus!" Men like Benny Hinn and Todd White, whom my youth pastor would have called heretics and charlatans, now enjoy a leading role in mainstream Evangelical youth movements.

The Send is orchestrated by several organizations but the founding entities are YWAM, and Lou Engle Ministries. The Send's website states that in the beginning "each leader grabbed hands making a commitment to do whatever it would take to see the re-evangelization of America and the finishing of the Great Commission." To get a better idea of "whatever it takes" might look like, let's examine the two organizations mentioned above.

YWAM's squalid history and deep DC connections have already been touched upon, but what was YWAM's mission in the first place? Its creator, Loren Cunningham, and the founder of Cru, Bill Bright, devised a strategy to rid the planet of secular society and thus hasten the end of the world. They believe that by dominating the world's "seven spheres, or mountains, of societal influence" they will have fulfilled the necessary biblical prophecies for Christ's return. Good ol' fashion millennialism. The Seven Mountains are: Religion, Family, Education, Government, Media, Arts & Entertainment, and Business. The Seven Mountain Mandate has been tacitly adopted throughout Evangelicalism, perhaps best demonstrated when the SBC called for America to "pray for the seven centers of influence" during the 2021 National Day of Prayer. They conveniently merged the mountains of "Entertainment" and "Media" to make room for the new mountain of "Military."

Fellow Dominionist, Seven Mountains man, and hobbiest

shouter Lou Engels is best known for his international campaigns against LGBTQ and abortion. While in Uganda in 2011 he promoted their "kill the gays bill," praising the country for its "courage" and "righteousness." In 2007 he sent his son to "cast out homosexual spirits" in San Francisco. Lou called for Christian martyrs in the fight against legalized abortion during his San Diego 2008 pro-Proposition 8 TheCall event. TheCall was the predecessor to The Send and was Lou's baby. TheCall was a massively attended youth event hosted around the world and served as his conduit to the seats of power wherever he visited. Funded in part by the incredibly terrifying National Christian Foundation (NCF), Lou used and was used by his connections to the Fellowship, the NCF, and other religious-right organizations to spread Christian nationalist politics around the globe.

As in the 50s and 60s a new push has begun for the soul of America's youth. Recognizing they are losing ground culturally Christian nationalists are allocating a massive amount of funds to these youth events and parachurch organizations. The Send, an event which filled three different stadiums, hosted bands, entertainers, and flew in speakers from all over the world, was absolutely free to attend. An amount of money that was once only dropped to buy campaigns or lobby Congress is now being thrown at men in tight shirts and dreadlocks. Each successful convert will be paying dividends for years to come.

It is hard not to sound conspiratorial when discussing the massive network of right-wing organizations "pulling strings" in DC. But I have recently uncovered that even I have a connection to the Fellowship. One that stretches back to early mornings spent at Burger King. Discussing the Netflix series *The Family* with Vulture Magazine in 2019, the author of *The Family and C Street,* Jeff Sharlet, exposed that connection when he said:

Jesse [creator of the Netflix series] made the right choice in not focusing on the homoeroticism of it, but it's pretty pervasive, right down to former Senator Sam Brownback, who's now Trump's ambassador for international religious freedom, telling me that his prayer cell would discuss their sexual feelings. A bunch of congressmen getting together to talk about how they struggle with masturbation, you can say that's silly and goofy and innocuous. I would argue that is in keeping with that mega-Christian right best seller, *Every Man's Battle* — the battle is supposedly with masturbation. There's another best seller, *Every Woman's Battle*, and every woman's battle is basically to keep her man sexually satisfied. There's a real stark divide there. Those things play out in the world and that's why it matters.

Several years and a dozen countries after sailing to South America, I found myself married and living in Atlanta, Georgia. I was working at another zoo and at another group home. My wife, Anna, was in grad school while working as a NICU nurse.

I was head over heels, but the early days of our marriage were rocky. We didn't date before we made the decision to get married. It wasn't some *I Kissed Dating Goodbye* situation. We would have dated, but we were rarely in the same country and neither of us were fully aware exactly when our friendship had crossed over into something much more.

Anna and I met 5 years earlier when I was visiting my friend Mike at Camp Rivercrest. Yes, the same "shout about Lance's masturbation" Camp Rivercrest. Mike was working as the head counselor and told me about Anna earlier in the week when I asked him about the girls working there that summer. He said there was a little Southern girl who everyone was into but he didn't really see it. I could see it, but the attraction wasn't reciprocated. We became friends and pen pals. I would write to her from almost every country I landed in and, occasionally, she would write back. She did not grow up with a conventional Evangelical upbringing but her religious beliefs were fairly traditional.

I was working in Laos when the realization hit. I was in love with her. Like, write awful love letters quoting Keats and Shelley kind of in love. I called her and she felt similarly. Tunnel vision is an expected symptom when you're falling hard. I was no exception. No longer having enough bandwidth to contemplate my religious uncertainties they were simply banished for the time being. Thus, my convictions conveniently began to parallel hers.

The next month I flew to Atlanta. Three weeks later my friend got ordained online and married us in Costa Rica. There were only the four of us in attendance; Anna, myself, Mike, who married us, and Anna's friend Laura, who served as witness. The whole ordeal was obviously rather impromptu. We decided on the location a day before the ceremony. It was a lovely hospedaje called The Lucky Bug in Nuevo Arenal. At the center of the property was a small private lake with a single dock. We were married at the end of the pier as the sun began to set.

When we got back to Atlanta I didn't have a job and had plenty of time on my hands, which led to spending far too much time browsing YouTube and Reddit. That's where I first tumbled down an Alt-Right rabbit hole. It started harmlessly enough, with interesting videos exploring the history of Western civilization. Within weeks I was watching videos claiming a white genocide was underway in America.

I leaned libertarian from early on, and there was an unending deluge of content targeting my exact biases. By clicking on "related videos," YouTube fed me a narrowing selection of content. Lectures by Milton Friedman shifted into Dennis Pragur, then Ben Shapiro and Steven Crowder. My history videos started with John Green's Crash Course, but somehow slipped to Carl Benjamin's Sargon of Akkad and on to Gavin McInnes. I started watching Tim Pool's reports and even endured

Milo Yiannopoulos on occasion. By the time Jordan Peterson and Dave Ruben gained popularity they felt like breaths of fresh air compared to the fetid vapors I had been breathing. I wasn't exactly adopting the Alt-Right talking points as my own; however, the programming from my childhood made me extra susceptible to the "suppressed" knowledge that was on offer.

Preferential access to secret wisdom is an intoxicating experience. Sadly, the validity of the facts is not as important as the associated feeling of being smarter than everyone else. I felt this addiction to arcana and pathos on two fronts, from my Dispensational Evangelical upbringing and from a growing conspiratorial mind. When you grow up believing that the Devil is constantly trying to rend you from your convictions and that faith is the highest virtue, it becomes second nature to interpolate those beliefs. Growth takes on a sinister hue. Accepting a thing as true without substantial evidence becomes a regular affair, and the dogmatic devotion once reserved for the numinous begins to encompass a wider and wider ambit. In short, a lifetime of positively knowing the unknowable tends to make one a touch more susceptible to bullshit.

Critical review is rarely an undesirable exercise. Particularly when tracing the culms and tendrils in your own thinking. (If only George Lucas had engaged in some critical review before attempting to breathe new life into a beloved classic.) It would have been easy for me to slip further, as so many others did, into a conspiratorial cesspool of Alt-Right mania. However, a few things stood in the way of that eventuality. One was Anna and her cool, but not dispassionate, logic. While neither history, political theory nor sociology were interests of hers, she can fish out an anachronism from any jumble of those practices. Another stemmed from my travels around the world. Having seen all that I had, very little of what these YouTube pundits had to offer jived with my experiences. Sure, their claims of oppression at the hands of a global leftist elite did make me homesick, but there was a general lack of substance and none of the nationalist jingoism was relatable. I had been to those places and met the "invaders" on whom they blamed the demise of Western civilization. Invaders or not, I found them quite pleasant.

Perhaps the tallest hurdle on my track to the right was how much I hate being wrong. I genuinely hate it. When confronted with my own wrong thinking, I often react negatively with loathsome defensiveness which will gradually transition into secret gratefulness for the new information. The duration of that transition depends on how wrong I was to begin with and who it was that brought it to my attention. Not my finest trait to be sure, but preferable to my traditional approach: ignore actual facts and make up my own. After so much of what I was watching on YouTube seemed to fall short of a logical conclusion or would butt up against my lived experience, my hatred of being wrong compelled me to search out opposing information. Quickly, the pinpricks I had noticed grew into massive holes.

My quest for perspective eventually led to enrolling in college 11 years after I had graduated from high school. I received my degree in International Studies. In my post-graduate studies I attained a teaching certification for history and social studies. In a roundabout way, I have right-wing shills and fake universities like Pragur U to thank for launching my actual education.

Dipping my toes into the Alt-Right swamp also had the added benefit of tugging my religious quandaries back to the forefront. What exactly the Alt-Right really is or was can be difficult to nail down. In my experience, Alt-Right is an umbrella term for a wide range of right-wing ideologies. Everyone from ultra-religious Neo-Nazis to atheist libertarian anarchists to angry incels could find a place there. The crossover in this Venn diagram of petulance was anti-feminism, anti-LGBTQ, and anti-internationalism. It was listening to a few of the more reasonable atheist libertarian anarchists that put me back in conflict with God. I slowly abandoned the talking heads and sought after the thinkers whom they referenced. I read a bit of Spinoza, Hume, and Hegel. I discovered that people had seriously been misrepresenting Adam Smith and Nietzsche. I found that the words of Engels and Rosa Luxemburg, not Friedman or Ayn Rand, best described the socioeconomic failures I saw all around me. A new world of thought opened up to me and the whole question of God's goodness or even his existence mattered slightly less. Every revolution does indeed have a counter-revolution, and in my case, the counter was the stronger.

My departure from guilt-ridden Evangelicalism has resulted in a much more profound joy than I had ever experienced from on high. My escape from fundamentalism has allowed for a greater appreciation of the wonders and complexities that the universe has on display. One such wonder arrived on April 27, 2020 at 3am. I started writing her a letter only a few hours before she arrived. I am adding it here as I find it a fitting mile marker to the evolution of which I have been writing. I was inspired by and quote Salman Rushdie's article *Imagine No Heaven*, which I had read a few days earlier while trying to prepare for my impending fatherhood.

Dear Fiadh,
You are likely to be the 7,780,800,001st person born on this planet. You will be making your screaming entrance in the next several hours, and as I sit here watching your mother try and rest, I cannot help but imagine the world you grow up to inhabit. With any luck, it will be a bit better than the one you will be born into. April 26, 2020, we find ourselves dead center of a pandemic and with the country being run by a charlatan who half the nation considers to be Elijah reborn. If, as you grow older, this planet grows more unstable, I am sorry. We are already on the verge of ecological disaster, fascist insurrection, and the resurfacing of religious tyrannies. Despite all this, the world still abounds with joy,

love, beauty, and human decency. Growing up here will require an open eye for both realities.

Soon you will be asking the same questions we have all asked. "Why am I here?" Beware of those who offer a ready answer. They all too often rely on the inexplicable, obfuscated, arcane, and the sacred. There is no panacea, and take note of those selling solutions that claim finality. There is reasonable conjecture to be found, but do not hesitate to throw out what you once believed in exchange for fuller truth.

Twenty-one years and a couple billion people ago, a much better man than I wrote this about another recently born child, "Live in your own time, use what we know and, as you grow up, perhaps the human race will finally grow up with you and put aside childish things." Allow your life to be an unending debate filled with greys and fuzzy answers. Life will wash over you, and in time some of those answers may sharpen as will your wit, humor, and conscience.

I promise to be a poor example of my ideals. I will be dogmatic without cause and self-assured when I should not be. However, I will never shut the doors of inquiry to you, and I will always encourage you to question with logic, reason, and yes, emotion. A last bit of unasked advice: never be a spectator to injustice or cruelty and never surrender your mind to any form of absolutism.

You were born before I could finish this letter. For a time there, I thought you were not going to survive the affair, and my heart broke with absolute sorrow. Up to that moment, I did not know I really wanted to be a father, but now I know I want to be your father. I love you terribly. So, I'll take this last line to introduce myself, my name is Lance, and I am your dad.

From before the Great Awakening and past the election of Ronald Reagan, Evangelicalism was molded over centuries and by millions of hands. Hands like those of Whitefield, Horace Bushnell, Billy Graham, and Rushdoony. I find myself relying on an old Youth Group analogy to best describe the current state of Evangelicalism. "Imagine a rose passed from hand to hand; with each pass, a petal is taken. In no time at all, the rose is nothing but a stem, and who would want to keep only a thorny stem?"

Thank you for purchasing *Youth Group: Coming of Age in the Church of Christian Nationalism*. My sincere hope is that you enjoyed reading this book and maybe even learned a thing or two. If you have a few moments, please feel free to add a review of the book at your favorite online site. Also, if you would like to connect with me or check out other upcoming books, please visit my website and don't forget to sign up for my newsletter: http://www.lanceaksamit.com

Sincerely, Lance Aksamit

Further Reading

If you enjoyed what you have read here and would like to read a few articles, poems, and books which helped me along the way, check out these titles:

Profit Over People Profit Over People: Neoliberalism and Global Order

by Noam Chomsky

Talking to My Daughter About the Economy: or, How Capitalism Works – and How It Fails

by Yanis Varoufakis

American Fascists: The Christian Right and the War on America

by Chris Hedges

How Jesus Became God: The Exaltation of a Jewish Preacher from Galilee

by Bart D. Ehrman

Exiting the Vampire Castle

by Mark Fisher

A Short History of Nearly Everything

by Bill Bryson

Dulce et Decorum Est

by Wilfred Owen

CULTURE, SOCIETY & POLITICS

Contemporary culture has eliminated the concept and public figure of the intellectual. A cretinous anti-intellectualism presides, cheer-led by hacks in the pay of multinational corporations who reassure their bored readers that there is no need to rouse themselves from their stupor. Zer0 Books knows that another kind of discourse - intellectual without being academic, popular without being populist - is not only possible: it is already flourishing. Zer0 is convinced that in the unthinking, blandly consensual culture in which we live, critical and engaged theoretical reflection is more important than ever before.

If you have enjoyed this book, why not tell other readers by posting a review on your preferred book site.

You may also wish to
subscribe to our Zer0 Books YouTube Channel.

Bestsellers from Zer0 Books include:

Give Them An Argument
Logic for the Left
Ben Burgis
Many serious leftists have learned to distrust talk of logic. This is
a serious mistake.
Paperback: 978-1-78904-210-8 ebook: 978-1-78904-211-5

Poor but Sexy
Culture Clashes in Europe East and West
Agata Pyzik
How the East stayed East and the West stayed West.
Paperback: 978-1-78099-394-2 ebook: 978-1-78099-395-9

An Anthropology of Nothing in Particular
Martin Demant Frederiksen
A journey into the social lives of meaninglessness.
Paperback: 978-1-78535-699-5 ebook: 978-1-78535-700-8

In the Dust of This Planet
Horror of Philosophy vol. 1
Eugene Thacker
In the first of a series of three books on the Horror of Philosophy,
In the Dust of This Planet offers the genre of horror as a way of
thinking about the unthinkable.
Paperback: 978-1-84694-676-9 ebook: 978-1-78099-010-1

The End of Oulipo?
An Attempt to Exhaust a Movement
Lauren Elkin, Veronica Esposito
Paperback: 978-1-78099-655-4 ebook: 978-1-78099-656-1

Capitalist Realism
Is There No Alternative?
Mark Fisher
An analysis of the ways in which capitalism has presented itself
as the only realistic political-economic system.
Paperback: 978-1-84694-317-1 ebook: 978-1-78099-734-6

Rebel Rebel
Chris O'Leary
David Bowie: every single song. Everything you want to know,
everything you didn't know.
Paperback: 978-1-78099-244-0 ebook: 978-1-78099-713-1

Kill All Normies
Angela Nagle
Online culture wars from 4chan and Tumblr to Trump.
Paperback: 978-1-78535-543-1 ebook: 978-1-78535-544-8

Cartographies of the Absolute
Alberto Toscano, Jeff Kinkle
An aesthetics of the economy for the twenty-first century.
Paperback: 978-1-78099-275-4 ebook: 978-1-78279-973-3

Malign Velocities
Accelerationism and Capitalism
Benjamin Noys
Long listed for the Bread and Roses Prize 2015, *Malign Velocities*
argues against the need for speed, tracking acceleration
as the symptom of the ongoing crises of capitalism.
Paperback: 978-1-78279-300-7 ebook: 978-1-78279-299-4

Meat Market
Female Flesh under Capitalism
Laurie Penny
A feminist dissection of women's bodies as the fleshy fulcrum of capitalist cannibalism, whereby women are both consumers and consumed.
Paperback: 978-1-84694-521-2 ebook: 978-1-84694-782-7

Babbling Corpse
Vaporwave and the Commodification of Ghosts
Grafton Tanner
Paperback: 978-1-78279-759-3 ebook: 978-1-78279-760-9

New Work New Culture
Work we want and a culture that strengthens us
Frithjof Bergmann
A serious alternative for mankind and the planet.
Paperback: 978-1-78904-064-7 ebook: 978-1-78904-065-4

Romeo and Juliet in Palestine
Teaching Under Occupation
Tom Sperlinger
Life in the West Bank, the nature of pedagogy and the role of a university under occupation.
Paperback: 978-1-78279-637-4 ebook: 978-1-78279-636-7

Color, Facture, Art and Design
Iona Singh
This materialist definition of fine-art develops guidelines for architecture, design, cultural-studies and ultimately social change.
Paperback: 978-1-78099-629-5 ebook: 978-1-78099-630-1

Sweetening the Pill
or How We Got Hooked on Hormonal Birth Control
Holly Grigg-Spall
Has contraception liberated or oppressed women?
Sweetening the Pill breaks the silence on the dark side of hormonal
contraception
Paperback: 978-1-78099-607-3 ebook: 978-1-78099-608-0

Why Are We The Good Guys?
Reclaiming Your Mind from the Delusions of Propaganda
David Cromwell
A provocative challenge to the standard ideology that Western
power is a benevolent force in the world.
Paperback: 978-1-78099-365-2 ebook: 978-1-78099-366-9

The Writing on the Wall
On the Decomposition of Capitalism and its Critics
Anselm Jappe, Alastair Hemmens
A new approach to the meaning of social emancipation.
Paperback: 978-1-78535-581-3 ebook: 978-1-78535-582-0

Enjoying It
Candy Crush and Capitalism
Alfie Bown
A study of enjoyment and of the enjoyment of studying. Bown
asks what enjoyment says about us and what we say about
enjoyment, and why.
Paperback: 978-1-78535-155-6 ebook: 978-1-78535-156-3

Ghosts of My Life
Writings on Depression, Hauntology and Lost Futures
Mark Fisher
Paperback: 978-1-78099-226-6 ebook: 978-1-78279-624-4

Neglected or Misunderstood
The Radical Feminism of Shulamith Firestone
Victoria Margree
An interrogation of issues surrounding gender, biology, sexuality, work and technology, and the ways in which our imaginations continue to be in thrall to ideologies of maternity and the nuclear family.
Paperback: 978-1-78535-539-4 ebook: 978-1-78535-540-0

How to Dismantle the NHS in 10 Easy Steps (Second Edition)
Youssef El-Gingihy
The story of how your NHS was sold off and why you will have to buy private health insurance soon. A new expanded second edition with chapters on junior doctors' strikes and government blueprints for US-style healthcare.
Paperback: 978-1-78904-178-1 ebook: 978-1-78904-179-8

Digesting Recipes
The Art of Culinary Notation
Susannah Worth
A recipe is an instruction, the imperative tone of the expert, but this constraint can offer its own kind of potential. A recipe need not be a domestic trap but might instead offer escape – something to fantasise about or aspire to.
Paperback: 978-1-78279-860-6 ebook: 978-1-78279-859-0

Most titles are published in paperback and as an ebook. Paperbacks are available in traditional bookshops. Both print and ebook formats are available online.
Follow us at:
https://www.facebook.com/ZeroBooks
https://twitter.com/Zer0Books
https://www.instagram.com/zero.books